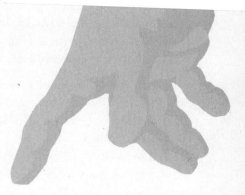

PROFOUND GOOD

BLAKE K. HEALY

CHARISMA
HOUSE

Most CHARISMA HOUSE BOOK GROUP products are available at special quantity discounts for bulk purchase for sales promotions, premiums, fund-raising, and educational needs. For details, write Charisma House Book Group, 600 Rinehart Road, Lake Mary, Florida 32746, or telephone (407) 333-0600.

PROFOUND GOOD by Blake K. Healy
Published by Charisma House
Charisma Media/Charisma House Book Group
600 Rinehart Road
Lake Mary, Florida 32746
www.charismahouse.com

This book or parts thereof may not be reproduced in any form, stored in a retrieval system, or transmitted in any form by any means—electronic, mechanical, photocopy, recording, or otherwise—without prior written permission of the publisher, except as provided by United States of America copyright law.

Unless otherwise noted, all Scripture quotations are taken from the Holy Bible, New International Version®, NIV®. Copyright © 1973, 1978, 1984, 2011 by Biblica, Inc.® Used by permission of Zondervan. All rights reserved worldwide. www.zondervan.com. The "NIV" and "New International Version" are trademarks registered in the United States Patent and Trademark Office by Biblica, Inc.®

Scripture quotations marked ESV are from the Holy Bible, English Standard Version. Copyright © 2001 by Crossway Bibles, a division of Good News Publishers. Used by permission.

Scripture quotations marked MEV are from the Modern English Version. Copyright © 2014 by Military Bible Association. Used by permission. All rights reserved.

Scripture quotations marked NASB are from the New American Standard Bible, copyright © 1960, 1962, 1963,

1968, 1971, 1972, 1973, 1975, 1977, 1995 by The Lockman Foundation. Used by permission. (www.Lockman.org)

Visit the author's website at blakekhealy.com.

Library of Congress Cataloging-in-Publication Data:
An application to register this book for cataloging has been submitted to the Library of Congress.
International Standard Book Number: 978-1-62999-565-6
E-book ISBN: 978-1-62999-566-3

While the author has made every effort to provide accurate internet addresses at the time of publication, neither the publisher nor the author assumes any responsibility for errors or for changes that occur after publication. Further, the publisher does not have any control over and does not assume any responsibility for author or third-party websites or their content.

19 20 21 22 23 — 987654321
Printed in the United States of America

CONTENTS

FOREWORD

IN PAST GENERATIONS THE LORD poured out His anointing
on individuals so that His goodness and power would be
displayed to His people. Entire generations were impacted
by the likes of Smith Wigglesworth, John G. Lake, Kathryn
Kuhlman, and countless others. People came from around
the world to receive from their ministries and to experience the presence and works of God for themselves. These
heroes of the faith were amazing gifts to the church. But
in recent days there has been a shift. It's not that God has
withheld His anointing from individuals. It's that He is
now pouring out His anointing on individuals who are
positioned to equip a generation. God's desire is for His
entire body to manifest His power and love, reaching the
whole world through the beauty of the gospel.

Blake Healy is one of these empowering individuals.
His focus is not only on what God has for him individ-
ually. It is also on the awakening of the body of Christ,
that it might reach its full potential. In his book *Profound
Good*, Blake takes us through his journey as a seer. I loved
his first book, *The Veil*, so much that I could hardly put it
down. It was one of those books that I felt disappointed to
finish. *Profound Good* is the same. His encounters with
the spirit realm are both moving and mind-boggling, but
ultimately they will leave you hungry for more of God.
This book is not just the memoir of a gifted man; it is the

journey of a teacher. With genuine humility Blake allows us to experience his learning curve as he expresses the reality of the spirit realm in a way that invites others to encounter God more fully. The kindness and generosity of the Father are at the core of this journey. As we read of Blake's unexaggerated visions and encounters with the Lord, we get to see a man who isn't growing just in his ability to see but also in his understanding of God's heart for His people.

We have been called to be naturally supernatural. In Matthew 5 there is an interesting verse. It says, "Pray for those who spitefully use you and persecute you, that you may be sons of your Father who is in heaven" (vv. 44–45, MEV). This doesn't mean that you become born again once you pray for someone who opposes you. It implies that when you do what is unnatural to people but natural for God, you step into who you are. And when you step into who you truly are, He is revealed. Nowhere is this more evident than in how we interact with the realm of the unseen.

We were born into a battle. We don't focus on the enemy. But to live without an awareness of the spiritual battle around us would be to limit ourselves to "acting like mere humans" (1 Cor. 3:3). Once we are born again, God's divine nature is within us. It is no longer acceptable to live within the limitations of humanity. God expects more; He anticipates more. He doesn't do this as an angry Father who is hard to please. He is well aware of what Jesus accomplished for us. Unfortunately we are just not always aware of it...yet. If you don't know you have money in the bank, you probably won't write checks. The discovery of what He's put into our account increases our capacity to live with risk that He might be known for who He is. We have been called to live a life that is unnatural for people but natural for God. And because we know what He's paid for, we can know what is possible through Him.

This book is a gift to the body of Christ. I can't imagine anyone reading through *Profound Good* without being stirred up with a fresh hunger for what is to be the "normal" Christian life. The insights gained will last a lifetime. The stories of Blake's encounters are not written to add shock value. Instead, they are included that they might reveal the Father in a way that compels us to love the world as He does. It is a world that cries out to experience God's true nature as a Father.

Blake successfully writes in a way that helps us understand it is not about his gift or call in life. In fact, he states, "I cannot see in the spirit because I am a gifted person. I can see in the spirit because I have a heavenly Father who wants me to know Him. That is why I can see in the spirit; that is why you can see in the spirit." The rich conclusion of *Profound Good* is that Blake Healy writes as a prophetic prototype of a generation to come. May it be us. May it be now.

—BILL JOHNSON
BETHEL CHURCH, REDDING, CALIFORNIA
AUTHOR, *WHEN HEAVEN INVADES EARTH* AND
THE WAY OF LIFE

INTRODUCTION

I WOKE UP THIS MORNING to the sound of my daughter, November, wiggling around in her crib. My wife got up with her the past few mornings, so I decided it was probably my turn. I looked out the window. It was still dark but in that warmish blue way it is just before dawn. I threw off the covers, rolled to my feet, and walked around to the crib, doing my best not to trip as I navigated the short obstacle course of laundry and plastic toys on the floor.

An angel was floating over my daughter's crib. It lay facedown in the air, looking at November face to face as it hovered two feet above her. The angel had long golden-blond hair and was wearing a purple-and-blue robe patterned with hand-stitched silver stars. The stars ran down along the surface of the fabric and fell off its edges, pouring down over the face of the smiling infant in the crib, along with a gentle flow of liquid light.

I have seen angels wearing similar robes in the past, and most of the time the Holy Spirit told me that the starry robes represent an impartation of wisdom. I felt the same impression as I looked at the angel floating over my daughter.

Once November noticed me standing over her, she reached up with her pink hands, breaking eye contact with the angel. I picked her up and carried her downstairs to make breakfast. As I made my way down, I saw a protection angel standing next to the front door. He has been

1

standing in the same spot ever since we moved into this house, stalwart and constant. He holds a tall spear in his right hand and wears silver-plated armor. His armor looks like something out of the Middle Ages but less heavy and bulky. His expression made it look as if he were staring at something a hundred miles away. He did not make eye contact as I walked by, but he never does. Protection angels are nothing if not intent.

I walked into the kitchen, put November in her high chair, and placed a small handful of cereal on her tray. I opened the refrigerator and browsed breakfast options, finally deciding on eggs and toast. I was humming a worship song as I closed the refrigerator, so I was not surprised to see a half dozen sparkling lights drifting around me in rhythm with my voice. The lights traced simple patterns of color in the air as I continued humming my mostly in-tune song. Whether these small balls of light are angels, heavenly hosts, or something else, I cannot say. They are things that are attracted to the presence of God, no matter how pronounced or subtle it is. Any more specific definition I've tried to give them has felt at least partially incorrect.

Each of the lights was a slightly different shade of yellow, and the patterns they made left short streaks of light that hung in the air for a few moments before vanishing. The pattern of their little dance was consistent but shifted in shape and tempo as I hummed my way from verse to chorus and back to verse again. I was sure that the patterns meant something—I believe every detail I see in the spirit does—but experience has taught me that unless my curiosity or the presence of the Holy Spirit is leading me otherwise, trying to discern the meaning behind every button on every angel's shirt or the purpose of every fluctuation of an angel's wings is the short path to frustration. There is deep meaning in it all, but only the guiding hand of the Holy Spirit can lead us to it.

I started cooking the eggs; scrambled was all I was ambitious enough to attempt this early in the morning. I'm mediocre at making omelets when I'm at the top of my game, and November was not going to be satisfied with staying in her chair for long. I looked over at her and saw her personal angel playing with her hair and tickling her nose. November laughed at every playful poke and reached out to grab at the angel's blond curls. I figured I had at least a few more minutes.

As the eggs continued to cook, I ran around the house, grabbing things I would need for the rest of the day. I am about as good at remembering everything I need for a day's work as I am at making omelets. November started to cry, upset that I kept leaving the room, so I picked her up and carried her around with me as I packed my things. Trying to carry my energetic infant along with my computer bag, notebook, and coffee tumbler quickly became more than my arms and hands could manage, so I set November down in the living room near a small basket of toys, which she promptly dumped over.

I then began running the day's events through my head. I had to drop my oldest son, Haydon, off at school at nine, and then I needed to head straight to the office for a meeting. My two-month-old son, Finnley, had a doctor's appointment after that, and I was sure I had made plans to meet someone after lunch… Then I started to smell burning eggs.

I am not sure if it was the harsh smell or because I had taken too long to get her more food, but my daughter began to fuss and whine. I snatched her up in one arm, cringing as I stepped on a small pile of surprisingly sharp toys, and continued into the kitchen to see how bad the damage was.

I did my best to salvage as much of the scrambled eggs as I could while also blocking my daughter's attempts to snatch the hot pan out of my hands. My back started feeling sore from carrying November around all morning, and I began feeling sorry for myself because of my failed attempt at making breakfast for everyone. I now needed to figure out another food plan in half the time.

I felt my frustration begin to mount as the rest of my to-do list resounded like a chorus in my head. Then I began getting frustrated that I was getting frustrated—burned eggs and a delayed breakfast are hardly the worst of the world's problems. What right did I have to be moody? It was then I saw a demon come around the corner.

There wasn't much to it. The demon was a little under three feet tall with grayish skin and a potbelly. It had dark eyes and a blank expression as it shuffled forward, its pace and posture that of a toddler who has smelled something tasty.

I could have commanded it to leave. "In the name of Jesus be gone. I banish thee from my household," or something like that. But that would not really solve the problem.

The problem was in my head. The problem was that I had let my circumstances, as trivial as they were, determine my level of internal peace.

Then I found myself humming again, the same worship song I was humming before. I gave my head a little shake to clear it, smiled at my daughter, and went back to the refrigerator to get more eggs. The demon turned around and skittered away after that. The mind-set that attracted it was gone.

I hummed the song all the louder, proud of my minor victory. November's angel turned to me and gave a quick nod of approval.

Seeing in the Spirit

I have seen angels, demons, and other spiritual things for as long as I can remember. I see them with my eyes, the same way I would see you if you were standing in front of me right now. I did not understand what I was seeing for the first twelve years of my life, partially because I was raised in a home that did not have a context for the gifts of the Spirit and partially because what I saw did not seem out of place to my young mind. Angels in gold cloaks and demons with sharp fangs were just as commonplace as mailboxes, telephone poles, and vending machines. To me, they were no more unusual than anything else.

When I was twelve, my family started attending a church that taught about the gifts of the Spirit, praying for people to be healed, hearing the voice of God, and learning to follow the Holy Spirit. It was the first time I ever had a context for the things I saw and the first time I realized the things I saw might have some greater purpose.

I spent the following ten years trying and failing to make good use of what I saw. I made a lot of mistakes. I did a lot of growing. My first book, *The Veil*, is about how I learned to use the gifts God gave me and how I discovered the purpose behind the things I saw. This book is about where God led me from there and how you can go there too. It is about why I can see in the spirit and why you can too. And it is about what seeing in the spirit tells us about who God is and what He is ready to do.

I wrote my first book three times. With the first attempt I tried to create a clear outline of the purpose, function, and availability of the gift of seeing in the spirit. I used regular scriptural references to support my claims, detailed my understanding of the reason why each angel looked the way it did, and attempted to create a clear framework for how each thing I saw functioned and interacted with the other things I saw. It was thorough, meticulous, and almost completely worthless. It was dry, dense, and, worst of all, mind-numbingly boring. Ironically, in trying to be as clear as possible, I created a completely inaccurate view of the world of the spirit. I threw away everything and started over.

My second attempt did not go much better. I just could not figure out how to be clear, how to teach someone about the things I saw in a structured and orderly manner. It never came out right.

It was then the Holy Spirit said to me, "You are not trusting your readers."

"What does that mean?" I asked.

"You are not trusting them to learn."

A series of memories flashed through my mind as He spoke. I saw my first few months of trying to learn to use the things I saw. I saw all the times when I was younger and did not even understand that the things I saw were the result of a gift. I saw the hours and hours of questions and conversations between me and the Holy Spirit that led me, step by step, to begin to understand what I was seeing. And then I understood what He was saying.

Seeing in the spirit is not like watching a nature documentary. You do not get detailed explanations of every angel, demon, and spiritual thing you see. You do not get helpful references to expand on the background and history of every spiritual situation you encounter. In fact, more often than not you do not get much of an explanation at all. You just get something new to talk to the Holy Spirit about.

With these thoughts in my mind, I knew what kind of book I was supposed to write. That version of *The Veil* was not as straightforward and clean as its previous iterations. It was messy in places, nonlinear, and occasionally obtuse, but it was also the truest book I had ever written about seeing in the spirit.

I share this story with you because this book was written the same way. It is not as direct as it could be. There are many more stories than there are explanations and commentary. It is not full of scriptural references or defenses of the claims found within. It is, however, the best way I know to give you what seeing in the spirit has given me, and it is the best way I know to teach you to see in the spirit yourself.

People sometimes ask me if it is hard to see in the spirit.

They wonder if seeing demons is too scary or if seeing spiritual wounds is too painful. The truth is, though I have compassion when I see them, demonic torment and deep spiritual wounding do not bother me all that much. I can feel God's plan for each of these situations, and He does indeed have a perfect plan for each one. The hardest and most painful thing about seeing in the spirit is seeing how abundantly God pours out His goodness on His people and how much of that goodness falls to the ground, unclaimed because we do not know it is there or ignored because we do not believe it is meant for us.

I believe every Christian can see in the spirit. I believe we are all fundamentally designed to have communion with God and to see the works of His hand across all the earth, both in the physical and spiritual world. And I believe learning to see in the spirit is one of the best ways to learn to see His goodness.

In this book I hope to give you three keys to help you unlock the gift of seeing in the spirit for yourself: pursuit, revelation, and intent.

1. Pursuit

Diligent pursuit of God's gifts and consistent practice using them creates comfort with and confidence in what He is saying, while conditioning our minds to receive revelation. We pursue gifts we have yet to experience by studying them in God's Word, seeking impartation (through laying on of hands, reading books, and listening to teachings) from others who have had breakthroughs in these gifts, making the pursuit of these gifts a part of our conversation life with God, and practicing them to the best of our ability.

While we do not and could not earn spiritual gifts, we can grow and mature in our ability to use them to their fullest.

Much as a violinist spends hundreds of hours practicing to be able to pull every nuance out of each note he or she plays, we grow in our mastery of the gifts God has given us through practice. Just as the violinist's ability to get beautiful music from the violin is correlated with his or her mastery of that instrument, our ability to effectively use our God-given spiritual gifts is at least partially dependent on our mastery of them.

God gives His gifts freely, but we develop them with diligent pursuit and plenty of practice.

2. Revelation

Seeing what God is doing and hearing what He is saying are meant to transform the way we think and the way we act. Everything He does and everything He says *reveals* a part of who He is—revelation. The transformation that comes from seeing His works and hearing His voice prepares our hearts and minds to receive all that He has for us. Without this preparation we may not recognize Him or His works, even when they happen right in front of our faces.

We can practice hearing His voice and study His written Word all we want, but if we do not allow the revelation we find there to transform the way we think and act, then we will never grow the spiritual muscles to carry what He has for us.

3. Intent

It may seem extreme, even hyperbolic, to say that the gift of seeing in the spirit is available for every Christian.

That is because many of us misunderstand God's intent toward man. If we are meant to be only obedient servants, then it makes sense that we should only be equipped to do the tasks we have been assigned—no more, no less. If, however, we are meant to be sons and daughters, heirs and ambassadors of His kingdom, then it makes sense that we should be invited to know and be equipped for more than what falls within the boundaries of our specific assignment; we would need to understand how His kingdom works.

Our belief in God's intent toward us sets the standard by which we see the world and the way we see Him.

~

We will be diving into these concepts in greater detail in subsequent chapters, but as you read through the encounters and stories in this book, be looking for the seeds of these ideas. It is one thing for me to share the revelations I have found and another for you to discover them for yourself.

My last request before we move forward into anything else is that you read this book with the Holy Spirit near and by your side. He is a much better teacher than I ever could be, and getting closer with Him is much more valuable than anything you could find in this book. He is the Teacher, the Advocate, the One who will remind us of all God has taught us. Nothing I see in the spirit is as meaningful, powerful, or transformative as what the Holy Spirit says about the things I see. Seeing in the spirit, or any other spiritual gift, is all but meaningless without a connection to Him and His voice. Without a connection to God, every gift is at most a shadow of what it is intended to be.

So keep your ears open to His voice, your eyes open for the works of His hand, and your heart soft toward His. In this I hope that you will discover the same truth that I have—that God is not just good; He is goodness itself. He is profound good.

SEEING-IN-THE-SPIRIT TRAINING— DAY 1

I WALKED INTO THE BACK of the church feeling more confident and alive than I had in years. For the very first time in my twelve years of life, the dancing lights and streaks of color I saw flitting around the church sanctuary were a source of curiosity rather than confusion. My eyes naturally skimmed the room, taking in what was happening in the spirit.

A tall angel wearing a silver-and-gold robe stood behind the main worship leader as he strummed the first few notes of the night's worship set on his guitar. The vibration of the strings sent out hazy waves of glitter-laden mist that quickly moved from where the worship leader stood to fill the whole room with glistening light. Two more angels trailing lengths of crimson cloth behind them skipped through the air above the chairs where the rest of the congregation sat. The crimson cloth snagged on some invisible hooks or lines at intervals throughout the room, making the cloth look as if it had been artfully hung for a wedding, reunion, or some other special occasion. A half dozen more angels, each wearing brightly colored clothes, leaped into the room as the rest of the band joined with the worship leader and led the congregation into worship.

I started looking for a place to sit, excited to continue watching what was happening. I was especially excited since I actually had a context for what it all could mean. Settling into a seat near the back of the room, I could not help but reminisce about how just a few weeks earlier I was completely confused and frightened. But now I was elated and empowered by the things I saw.

I had always seen things other people did not—even my first memories are interlaced with visions of angels and demons—but it never caused much of a problem until I turned nine and the scariest things I had ever seen started visiting me on a nightly basis. Each night for three years I saw every kind of imaginable and unimaginable horror in full, 3-D living color. Though these terrors never invaded my day-to-day life, they were always there waiting when I went to lay my head on my pillow. I saw angels and demons during the day, but for some reason the demonic beings I saw during the day did not scare me at all, while the ones I saw at night left me so terrified I could hardly breathe. After trying everything I could think of to dispel or drown out these dark visions, I became resigned to the fact that I was either crazy or the devil had just decided to ruin my life—neither of which left much room for hope.

My salvation came suddenly and unexpectedly. We had only been attending our new church for a few weeks when one Sunday morning someone stepped on the stage to announce what he called a prophetic training class. "Learn to hear God's voice, and discover how He is speaking to you," he said. "Everyone is meant to hear His voice; anyone can learn to do it."

It sounded interesting, but not quite interesting enough for me to want to go to church twice in one week. My mom, however, was interested enough to make sure the whole family went together. I didn't know it at the time, but my whole life was about to change.

At the class they taught that God speaks in a variety of ways. He speaks through pictures in our mind's eye; dreams; impressions; His still, small voice; divine coincidences; and many, many more methods. They taught that we are all designed to hear God's voice and that He is always speaking—we only need to learn how to listen.

I sat and listened with my jaw on the floor. Though I realized around the age of eight or nine that other people were not seeing some of the things I saw, I never considered the possibility that what I saw could be because of a gift. By the time I realized I saw things differently than other people did, the nightly terrors had made me too frightened to share the full extent of what I saw with anyone. I had only told my parents that I was having nightmares.

The person teaching the class did not describe anything quite like what I was experiencing as he spoke about the prophetic gift, but the things he shared reminded me of things I had seen. It was only a start, but it was more context than I had ever had for the things I saw—enough that I was finally able to work up the courage to tell my parents exactly what was happening with me.

I told my parents, and together we went to share with the leaders of the prophetic ministry at the church. Though none of them had experienced the same things I had, they had at least heard of other people like me. Something changed in that moment. I don't know if it was because I finally shared what I was experiencing with someone else, or if it was the discovery that my nightly terrors were not caused by slipping sanity or simple demonic attack but were instead the result of a gift I had not yet learned to manage, but over the course of a week the nighttime fears completely ended. I still saw demons every night that week, but the wave of fear that used to accompany them was almost completely absent. By the end of the week they had stopped bothering to come at all.

So there I was, sitting at the back of the church, ready to learn how to use this gift God had given me: seeing-in-the-spirit training—day one.

The angels finished hanging the last of the red fabric around the sanctuary and then moved to the area in front of the stage and began dancing in perfect time with the worship team's music. The angel wearing gold and silver stood solemnly just behind the worship leader, and the glittering mist emanating from the worship leader's guitar continued to fill the room with sparkling light.

I saw a handful of other angels as I looked around the room. Most were either standing near one of the other people in attendance or dancing around the room. I saw little blurs of light in some places. I could see movement, but it was too unclear to discern much else. It looked like someone had smeared a handful of petroleum jelly over that part of the room, obscuring beyond recognition whatever was there.

I saw a large black snake at the back of the room. Its tree-trunk-sized coils were covered in dark, leathery scales, and its bright-yellow eyes were glowing as it lowered its head from where it hung high in the rafters. The familiar fear that had been such a consistent part of my nightly life scratched at the back of my head as I saw the snake, but the feeling was easily suppressed, especially when I noticed how hard the snake was pressing itself against the back wall, as if it were afraid to get any closer to what was happening at the front of the room.

I continued my survey of the sanctuary, trying to re-call more memories of seeing angels and demons from my past so I could apply my newfound understanding to the old experiences. When I was young, seeing in the spirit did not feel at all different from seeing in the natural. The angels and demons I saw on a daily basis fit naturally into the background of my daily life. Now that I was paying special attention to the things I knew were spiritual, even though I could see them as clearly as the person sitting in front of me, the spiritual things looked as if they were made of something else.

Everything moved a little differently than it would in the physical. The angels rose and fell as if gravity were an optional part of their dance. They glowed as if their skin and clothes were themselves a light source, rather than reflecting light from elsewhere in the room.

I never intentionally saw in the spirit when I was a child. It would just happen, naturally woven in with everything else I saw. Since I now knew what I had was a gift, I wondered if I could switch it on or off. Furrowing my brow in concentration, I gave it a try. It worked instantly. Like choosing to focus on one person rather than another or on something in your peripheral vision rather than something at the center of your vision, I was able to focus on the physical world, making everything spiritual fade away. With another adjustment I was able to focus on what was going on in the spirit.

I sat there for a moment, switching back and forth between the spirit and the physical. It took energy and focus to intentionally stay fixed on one or the other, similar to exercising an infrequently used muscle, but I could do it. I noticed that when I concentrated on the spirit, some of the spots that were merely blurs of light began to come into focus. A blur near the front door of the room resolved into an angel in shining silver armor standing sentinel with a longsword in his hand and a look of determination on his face. A greenish-blue smudge was actually a small childlike angel in a blue robe pouring a vase of green liquid onto the stage. The liquid flowed over the edge of the stage and spread across the room, covering the feet of everyone it passed with its emerald light. There were still several dozen blurry places around the room, but I could see much more when I remained fixated on the spirit.

And so it went, week after week, month after month. I looked and I saw. I watched and I learned. Progress was slow, but it was also steady. I understood the purpose of less than 10 percent of what I saw, but everything I saw added more notes to sections of my growing internal encyclopedia of the spirit realm.

One week I saw a fifteen-foot-tall figure made of milky light. I did not know why it was there or what it was doing, but it stood on the right side of the stage for the entire worship service. The next week, I saw the same figure of blurred light, but this time I could see its feet clearly. It was wearing jewel-encrusted sandals. What did this mean? What was its purpose? I had no idea, but it was a little more detail. The following week, I could see the angel's feet, legs, and hands. It wore rings on each of its fingers that matched the ornamentation on its sandals. It was holding a large golden staff with a square, shovellike platform at its apex. The following week, only the angel's face was still obscured. The angel was wearing a robe covered in gold and jewels that complemented the adornments on its feet and hands.

For the first time I could see what the angel was doing. It extended the staff toward the crowd of worshippers. As they sang and lifted their hands in praise, thin wisps of smoke emerged from their mouths and fingertips, swirling and flowing together as they moved forward and collected together in the shovel part of the angel's staff. Once it was full, the angel lifted the staff high into the air. The contents of the shovel burst into flame, burning hotter and hotter as the tempo of the worship music intensified. Then the angel flung the red-hot contents of the staff—a swirling cloud of embers—back into the crowd. The embers ignited the smoke still being released from the worshippers, whipping up a churning maelstrom of particulate light. All ose into the air in a rush that flowed perfectly with the crescendo of the music.

The response of my heart, matched with the violent beauty of the display, made the angel's purpose clear: it was here to increase our capacity to worship our God. The moment this thought entered my mind, the smear of light obscuring the angel's face cleared. It was the face of a man in his mid-forties. His skin tone and facial features did not evoke any specific ethnicity or race. This is not to say that he looked bland or featureless; in fact, as I looked at his expression as the next song began, I was shocked to see how much of this angel's personality and character came through his countenance.

The same procession of smoke gathering in the shovel, being ignited, and then being returned to the worshippers happened again almost exactly as it had during the first song, but seeing the look of sincere passion and commitment on the angel's face as he performed his duties made the entire experience even more overwhelmingly impactful. He was so intent on the service he was performing for the congregation and for the Lord that it convicted and inspired me to my very core.

Month by month my ability to focus on the things I saw grew more and more refined. I could choose to focus on what was happening around a specific individual or what was happening to the room as a whole. I could choose to look for the demonic or the angelic. I could choose to look for soul wounds in and on the people around me, or I could choose to look at the presence of God moving around them. I could choose to focus on people's prayers and how they shifted and made changes in the atmosphere, or I could focus on the worries and fears that popped around their heads like a mini fireworks display. Though I definitely did not understand everything I saw, I felt that I was beginning to understand some of how the spirit realm worked.

After a few months of practicing, I decided it was time to start sharing the things I saw. After all, why would God show me these things if He did not want me to share them with the people around me? I told the worship team about the kinds of angels I saw during worship that week, and I told my pastor about how the presence of God was moving around the room during his teaching. This always seemed to encourage them. Sometimes they had further questions about why a certain angel was doing this or why another angel was doing that. This usually made me anxious, since I generally only understood the bit I shared. Further details were either completely absent or like scattered puzzle pieces on the table of my brain; it usually took me several weeks to get a clear picture of how everything fit together.

I tried to tell people about the demonic things I saw on them, but this usually didn't go so well. Some people got very angry at me, some panicked, and some felt deeply ashamed when I told them about what I saw. It was hard to understand why people reacted so harshly. I did not feel angry at them when I saw a demon was trying to bother them. I was not scared of them, especially when I was talking to the Holy Spirit about what I saw. I didn't see why they should feel ashamed because of something a demon was trying to do.

21

Despite the bumps, the path ahead seemed clear. I was learning more and more about how the realm of the spirit worked, and I was learning how to use the things I saw. I knew I still had a lot to learn, but I was confident that God would show me how to use the things I saw for His glory.

PART I
Life on Earth

THE SPIRIT REALM IS AN intrinsic part of our daily lives. It is not a secret dimension we only access through spiritual rite or religious ritual; it is as fundamental to creation as the laws of science and mathematics that God designed as the background of our day-to-day human experience.

God's presence and plans extend well beyond the boundaries of our homes and churches. He is everywhere. Angels do not hide in church sanctuaries, waiting for the next Sunday service to come around; they go where we go, looking for ways to enact the purposes of God and support the ambassadors of His kingdom.

So what does that mean when I am at the grocery store? Or when I am picking up my kids from school? Or when I am waiting around in the doctor's office?

In the following section you will find stories about what happens in the spirit during the normal, the mundane, and the routine. Look for the significance that heaven places on your day-to-day journey and the value that God has for every detail of your life.

A DAY AT THE POOL

WE ARRIVED AT THE PUBLIC swimming pool with our arms full. I had bags overflowing with towels, flotation devices, bottles of water, and plenty of snacks. My wife, April, had our newborn, Finnley. Haydon, our three-year-old, was running ahead, desperate to spend every available second playing in the water. I followed close behind, eager to strap him into his life vest as soon as possible since three-year-olds are not the most buoyant things on the planet.

With our bags emptied and our chairs claimed with beach towels, Haydon and I jumped into the pool, while April and Finnley sat and played in the shade. April's angel, wearing a pink-and-white dress, knelt down just behind her. The angel was popping her head over April's shoulder periodically, making funny faces at the baby in a perfectly complementary rhythm with the funny faces and sounds April was making. I call April's angel "she," not because I think her angel is a girl, but because the angel's dress, long sandy-blond hair, and features all look feminine to me. I don't think angels are female and male, at least not in the same way we are, but I do often see them personifying more masculine or feminine traits.

Haydon and I swam all around the pool, splashing and playing. His angel stayed right by him for the majority of the time, leaving only occasionally to point out something interesting elsewhere in the pool. The angel would zip across the water with his green cloak flapping in the wind, then stop at a spot and flap his arms wildly. Haydon would then begin paddling in that direction. Sometimes we would find something interesting there, such as a small insect skating across the surface of the water; other times there would be nothing interesting as far as I could tell, though Haydon always found something fascinating about every location. We didn't go to every spot Haydon's angel pointed out; sometimes my toddler's natural curiosity took us in a different direction. The pool was large and winding, with little waterfalls and other fun features, so sometimes he just went after those.

I wondered as we paddled back over toward the side where April and Finnley were playing if Haydon could actually see his angel pointing out places for him to go, or if the way his personal angel interacted with him was so natural and familiar that it was all but indistinguishable from his own internal processes. Was the angel actually telling him where to go or just gently tugging on his childish curiosity? I would have just asked him, but it is challenging to get clear answers to these kinds of existential questions from a toddler.

~

We had the whole pool to ourselves for a while. After we had been playing for fifteen minutes or so, a woman in her sixties came to swim. She wore a navy blue one-piece bathing suit with white ruffles on the shoulders, a white ruffled swim cap, and a neon green diver's mask. She had bright orange inflatable children's water wings on both arms, three or four foam noodles tucked in the crook of her arm, and two small foam kickboards in her hand. As a child I was taught it is impolite to stare, but I was having a very hard time not staring at that particular moment.

Gingerly the woman lowered herself into the water, making sure none of her equipment got loose. She held on to the edge of the pool, tucked the noodles under both arms, and lay across both kickboards. She then dipped her face about two inches into the water, pushed off the wall, and started paddling. She made it about ten inches before she whipped her face out of the water and stood up, huffing, spitting, and sputtering. She straightened out the various implements that had gone astray during her journey and kicked her way back to the pool's edge. Before long she was all set up once more and launched into a second attempt. This time she paddled for at least a full twelve inches. Again, she came up coughing and sputtering, and again, she returned to the edge of the pool for another go. She went through this routine over and over and over again for forty-five minutes, never stopping for more time than it took to catch her breath.

Though I was doing my best to give her privacy, I couldn't help but be fascinated by what this woman was up to. Without really thinking about it, I looked in the spirit during one of her attempts. I saw her angel standing on the water over the woman as she pushed and paddled her way through the pool. Her angel could not have looked more excited. She was jumping up and down, pumping her fist, and shouting, "You got this! You can do it! Go! Go! Go!" Her angel looked like a parent watching his or her child score the winning goal during the championship game.

I looked a little to the right and saw a demon floating over the woman. It was short and spindly, with sharp, pointed fingers. Each time the woman dipped her head in the water and started paddling, the demon reached down, poking, jabbing, and scratching at the back of the woman's head. Though I could both feel and see the viciousness and disdain in the demon's action, when I looked at the demon's face, I didn't see a look of aggression but of sheer panic. It looked terrified.

Stepping back and looking at the scene as a whole—the woman swimming with all her might, with noodles and kickboards flopping everywhere; the angel dancing and cheering; and the demon scrabbling and scratching—I couldn't help but ask the Holy Spirit, "What's going on here?"

"She has been afraid of water since she almost drowned when she was three," He replied without hesitation, "but she decided today that it was time to get over that fear."

He spoke with a tone of such fatherly pride that I found myself speechless. It was so infectious that I found myself feeling proud of the woman myself—that she would be willing to put so much effort into overcoming something that surely must have become a normal part of her everyday life, that she would keep going and trying not for ten minutes but for forty-five, and that she would keep it up even though a three-year-old was literally swimming circles around her. I felt overwhelmed with joy at what she was doing.

After Haydon and I swam around for a while longer,

April waved me over so she could take a turn swimming. I hopped out of the pool and sat next to our newest baby, who was now sound asleep in a small portable crib.

April is much more personable than I am. I did my best to avoid staring too long at the woman in the navy blue bathing suit. I tried to keep Haydon from swimming over and bothering her. I tried to stay on one side of the pool so she could keep on with her practice without being disturbed.

The moment April saw the woman, what she was wearing, and all the equipment she had with her, she swam up to her and said, "Hey! What are you doing?"

The woman stopped, straightened her swim cap, laughed, and said, "You know, honey, I realized at the beginning of this year that I have way too many dreams to let fear hold me back from any one of them. So I decided that this year I am going to face every one of my fears. This week I'm learning to swim, and next week I'm going skydiving."

~

It's easy to believe God gets excited about the big things. It's easy to believe God is excited when you share the gospel with someone, when you pray for someone and he or she is healed, or when you give a prophetic word that brings insight and blessing to someone's life. It's easy to believe God would be excited if you gave all you had to the poor or moved to a third-world country to serve the people and His purpose there. But it is sometimes difficult to believe God is just as excited when you make it to work on time, when you replace the light bulb that has been out for a month, or when you have an opportunity to be harsh with your children but instead walk the path of peace. It's difficult to believe God is actually excited that you installed a key hook near your front door so you won't lose your keys as often, that you found a more efficient way to run the spreadsheet of your company's budget plan, or that you made muffins that taste really good. It's harder to believe those things could make God excited because we have an incomplete view of how great His love is.

Every victory is celebrated in the halls of heaven—no matter how big or how small. Why? Because every victory has reverberations that go so much further than we see. That woman was not just learning to swim—she was learning to overcome fear. Overcoming fear is a skill she can apply to other areas of her life. It is a skill she can teach others. The demon had a look of terror on its face because it was losing its place in her life. The little crevice of normalized fear that had been its hiding place was being filled in with boldness and courage. Getting over a fear of swimming may not be the most significant thing a person could do, but learning to get over fear is a victory that can change every part of your life.

Thoughts to Ponder

- The woman's angel was celebrating her victory over fear with great enthusiasm. What does this angel's behavior tell us about the kind of relationship personal angels have with their people?

- The demon was terrified to lose its place of influence in the woman's life. What does this suggest about its goals? What does it teach us about how to get rid of demonic influence in our lives?

- My wife, April, asked the woman a direct question. Do you think the story would have been as impactful if we did not know the background of why the woman was doing what she was doing? Learning to ask questions, and developing the boldness to actually ask them, is one of the quickest ways to grow in wisdom and revelation. *Jesus!*

Laurla said - dont know why people dont invite the angels more-

MUNICIPAL COURT

I HAD TO GO TO court a few years ago. I received a ticket for driving with an expired tag. My car had been having radiator problems for several months. I finally got around to fixing it, but I had not made it to the tag office to replace the tag, which expired while the car was broken down. I had a side job and was having a hard time finding a ride. Because I was running late for the job, I drove the car with the expired tag and ended up with a ticket. The terms listed on the ticket required that I go to the municipal court to plead my case and pay the fine.

So at six o'clock on a foggy, cold Tuesday morning I set out in my now perfectly street-legal car to enjoy some time at a small-town municipal court. I pulled up to the mostly gray and mostly square building just as the sun was finishing its climb over the horizon. After mistakenly entering a traffic class, a police training seminar, and a maintenance closet, I finally found the courtroom.

The room was completely packed, with every chair taken and every comfortable section of wall claimed. People of every shape, size, and color sat smashed together in tight rows, each fiddling with one of a variety of legal documents. A half dozen or so police officers were stationed at key points around the room, with two more standing at either side of a massive desk at the front of the room, where the judge and his staff sat in a long row. I found the least congested corner I could and wedged myself into it. My ideal day would probably consist mostly of reading by myself and spending some time with my wife and kids, maybe followed by a few close friends visiting after dinner. Being tightly packed into a room with way too many strangers who were all experiencing varying levels of indignation would not be high on my list of great ways to spend a day.

In situations such as these I generally turn off my ability to see in the spirit—it just gets too crowded. But soon boredom got the better of me, and I began looking in the spirit. There were 150 or so people, each with a personal angel, each of which was doing something specific and unique. Each person's thoughts, opinions, and attitudes were sending sparks and images into the room like mental exhaust. The room itself had its own set of angels that were not attached to any particular person; they were just part of the structure and flow of everything that happened there. Somewhere around twenty demons were meandering around the room, looking for opportunities. A flash of disappointment or frustration, concerns over finances or further legal trouble, a perceived slight from someone in the room—any of these could present the kind of opening that demons look for.

There was much more, of course, but it can be hard to know where to stop when describing things other people don't normally see. Imagine trying to explain what your living room looks like to a blind person. Do you keep things broad, merely saying there's a couch, a carpet, a TV, and a ceiling fan? Or do you delve into the most minute of details, describing the particular pattern and grain of the rug, the design and style of the coffee table along with what kind of wood it is made of, how many light bulbs are inside the lighting fixture hanging in the entryway, how many panes are in the windows, whether the curtains are drawn or closed, how many different pillows are on your couch, and how the intricately stitched patterns on the front of each are an expression of your shabby-chic style? Or do you go even further, detailing the history of why your living room looks the way it does—explaining how your dog chewed the corner of the couch when he was a puppy; how the coffee table belonged to your mother, who recently moved to a smaller house and could not find room for it; and how the carpet is white but you are hoping to change it soon because it is too much of a hassle to keep it clean with a dog and four kids in the house?

There is just as much, if not more, happening in the spirit realm. We all have an entire interconnected system of spiritual activity related to our history, our mind-set, our personality, and things that have happened during that particular day. These all form together into a kind of spiritual ecosystem, an amalgamation of everything that is attracted and created by the way we act, think, and believe. Every corner of our world is marked by the way we have lived in it—in good ways, bad ways, and some ways that are a mixture of both. In the spirit these marks, structures, and systems tell the story of our history and set the stage for our future. It can feel overwhelming when we realize how much of what we do and think impacts the world around us, which is why I am so glad that we have been given access to the guidance of the Holy Spirit.

~

Even as I found myself being overwhelmed with all that was going on just with the small slice of humanity found in the municipal courtroom, I began to feel the gentle tug of the guiding hand of the Holy Spirit. He drew my attention to a man sitting in the back row on the far side of the room. He had big, broad shoulders and was tapping both feet as his fingers drummed on the back of the document in his hand. I couldn't see what kind of paper it was from where I was sitting, but it had a lot of red lettering on the front. A demon was squatting down in front of the man, blowing on the back of the paper in his hand. The demon's breath released an ashy smoke that ran around the paper and into the man's eyes.

Each time a puff of the smoke went into the man's face, his eyes would dart from left to right nervously. Dark images appeared around his head. Snapshots of a car being repossessed, his wife looking disappointed, and the man asking his boss for more hours at work came out of his mind like smoky shadows.

His angel whipped out a sharp gold-plated sword with a red tassel hanging off the hilt—similar to the style of sword a samurai might have—and began slashing the shadowy images. The angel moved swiftly and precisely, striking each image only once. The demon began blowing harder, its expression growing more desperate. The angel moved even more quickly, matching the increased pace at which the dark images began appearing.

Suddenly the man stood up. He shook his hands as if he were trying to loosen them up, rolled his shoulders, and let out a deep sigh. He noticed an elderly woman leaning against the wall nearby and offered her his seat. She refused for a moment, but she eventually gave in to his insistence and sat down.

The demon followed him as he moved, huffing and puffing at the paper as it flapped around with the man's movement, but none of the smoke reached the man's face. As the man settled against the wall where the woman had been, I saw a small golden club appear in his angel's hand. The angel immediately batted the demon on the side of its head, sending it tumbling away.

"Why didn't the angel just do that right away?" I asked the Holy Spirit, speaking in my mind. "Why did he wait until the man got up?"

I didn't get a clear answer. I don't always. I just felt a gentle touch on certain parts of my memory of what had just transpired. The demon was blowing on the paper. I got the impression of blowing on embers to try to start a fire. The demon was trying to heighten the stress the man was feeling about whatever legal problem he was facing.

The shadowy images seemed to be coming from the man himself, but something about them did not look right. The scenes and facial expressions in the pictures looked slightly exaggerated. These worries and fears were coming from the man, but they were being twisted by what the demon was doing, making them seem much worse.

The angel was chopping at the thoughts but basically ignoring the demon. I got the impression of a police officer making an arrest: the need for strict protocol and procedure and having a set of standards regarding jurisdiction and authority. The angel had the authority to intervene with the shadowy thoughts but not the demon itself.

I lost track of what the demon and the angel were doing when the man stood up. I was distracted by his sudden movement. Maybe he was shaking himself out of his line of thinking.

It was not until he got out of his thought pattern that he noticed the older woman who was standing near him. By the way he insisted that she take his seat, it would be fair to assume it would have been in his character to give it to her much sooner if he had noticed she was there.

After all of this transpired, the angel received a new weapon. It appeared with a flash of light. The second he had the weapon, he immediately used it to dispatch the demon. Was it the act of kindness that made it possible for the angel to get rid of the demon?

I felt the sense of the guiding hand of the Holy Spirit lift. If it had made a sound, it would have been a record scratch. So I knew I missed something. I ran the whole thing through my head again—the demon blowing ash, the shadowy thoughts, the angel slicing thoughts away, the man standing up and giving away his seat, and the angel being equipped. The Holy Spirit took a step back when I started thinking that the act of kindness was what equipped the angel to get rid of the demon.

One sentence—not an audible statement but rather

a clear and succinct thought—ran through my brain: "Freedom from the influence of demons is normal."

His act of kindness did not "earn" him freedom from the demonic attack he was experiencing. He showed an act of kindness because he stopped focusing on the negative thought process he was stuck in. The angel did not have the authority to dispatch what the man was focusing on. As soon as he stopped focusing on the negative thoughts, or at least stopped focusing on them in the way the demon was trying to get him to, the angel was able to receive what he needed to get rid of the demonic influence. The man doing something kind for someone else was a natural side effect of his corrected mind-set.

My train of thought was interrupted by the huffy shouts of a man in the center of the room.

"Well no, I *don't* see how that's relevant." The man standing before the judge was shaking a handful of papers in the general direction of the panel of court staff.

"Sir," the judge responded, "regardless of how relevant you do or do not think it is, the fact remains that you were fishing without the proper license."

I had to reorient myself for a moment. I had become so engrossed in watching what was going on in the spirit that I had forgotten I was in a courtroom.

The defendant (a term I gleaned from watching 1990s police procedurals and that was possibly completely incorrect in this context) was wearing a red flannel shirt that closely matched the shade of crimson that spread across his face as he held back another outburst. His angel was standing next to him, massaging one of the man's shoulders in a calming gesture.

The judge also looked as though he was working hard to keep himself calm. His angel stood on his right, gently pouring a pitcher of water on the judge's head—not dumping it on him, just cooling him off a bit. Another angel stood behind the judge. This one was more than ten feet tall, covered in intricately detailed and beautiful golden ornaments and wearing similarly resplendent clothing. It was holding a thick golden scepter with a ruby affixed to the top. It had massive golden wings and piercing eyes that sometimes seemed red, sometimes green, and sometimes gold, depending on how I tilted my head. I caught myself using the pronoun *it* while making note of the angel's appearance in my mind. This struck me as strange. When I sat and thought about it, I definitely got an overall masculine impression from the way the angel looked, but something about the otherworldly way that the angel floated at the back of the courtroom made using the term *him* seem inappropriate.

The angel was not just there to perform a task or do a job. This angel *was* the thing it did. I knew without question it was an angel of justice. How did I know that? It really is hard to say. I often find that though I do not always immediately understand the things I see, most of what I see is familiar. I sometimes wonder if my spirit understands much more than my mind does. Maybe my spirit can see the abstract complexity of a heavenly being and easily derive meaning from it the same way my brain can almost instantly perform all the complex calculations necessary to catch a ball that has been thrown at me.

In the context of my mind I saw that every part of the angel was perfectly balanced. All the gold ornaments, the scepter, and the angel's massive wings looked incredibly heavy. Yet each part was perfectly balanced with the other parts. The angel appeared to be perfectly symmetrical, apart from the fact that it was only holding a scepter in one hand. The rest of its body, including its wings, adjusted to compensate for the imbalance in weight as the angel gently moved the giant scepter from left to right in a slow, sweeping motion, as if it were emphasizing a proclamation to the room at large. All these details were interesting on their own, but they did not necessarily evoke any clear meaning. However, the word *justice* kept ringing out from somewhere deep in my chest anytime I looked at the angel. The sound of that word gave accent, purpose, and character to every aspect of the angel's appearance.

The symmetry spoke of the flawless nature of heaven's justice. The scepter, a representation of authority and the ability to act on that authority, would have caused imbalance with every movement, but the angel easily compensated for the shifting weight. It was as if every part of the angel and what it was wearing was designed to accommodate the heavy movements of the scepter. I could not grasp all of the meaning behind what I was seeing other than a distant understanding that I was seeing a picture of how heaven's perfect justice interacts with an imperfect world.

I could feel that my spirit understood what I was

seeing, but in this case it was very challenging to resolve what my spirit knew with what my mind could comprehend. Maybe that is why I automatically used the word *it* to describe this angel. *He* was too down-to-earth a term for something that felt so far outside comprehension.

The man on the stand continued to plead his case, growing increasingly frustrated. His angel kept trying to calm him in different ways—patting his arm, rubbing his back, and things like that. It was then I noticed the demon floating in the air just in front of the man. It was like a featherless bird. It had a long, narrow beak; a scrawny black body; and thin, membranous wings. It floated in the air a few feet in front of the man's face with its wings spread wide. I noticed its wings were so thin that one could see through them, and everything looked very different when viewed through this dark lens.

When I looked at the faces of the court staff members through the demon's wings, their expressions looked subtly altered. Polite smiles and normal looks of concentration took on more sinister tones. Every smile looked like a smirk, every shrug sarcastic, every glance disdainful. Through this dark filter the judge looked older and more imperious. I could feel an involuntary distrust and suspicion rise in my throat. Even the angel looked completely different when I looked at it through the wings. Instead of gold, its ornaments were made of rough iron. Instead of a scepter, it held a blunt, misshapen hammer. Its deep, otherworldly face looked dull and brutish.

The demon was trying to shape the perspective of the man on the stand. Through this lens everyone was against him. Through this lens the only justice to be found was what he could grab out of the hands of the unjust.

I see this kind of thing all the time. One of the main things demons try to do is warp our perspective of people and the world around us. They try to take a minor slight and turn it into a major insult. They try to take disappointment and turn it into depression. They try to take the imperfections of others and turn them into irredeemable flaws.

I cannot be sure what caused this man to buy into the version of reality that the demon was trying to show. Maybe his past experience with the legal system gave him a perfectly understandable reason for distrust. Maybe his parents, intentionally or unintentionally, taught him to expect mistreatment from the government or authority in general. Maybe he was just really upset about the fine he had to pay and therefore ready to believe anything bad about those who were making him pay.

I was surprised to see that the demon's wings even made the angel look different. I had not seen that before, but it did make sense. I have seen people in the middle of a terrible argument, with a demon standing between them. When I would look at one person or the other through the demon, the individual's features would often be exaggerated, making the person look more imposing or spiteful. You can feel this happen when a small offense or misplaced word spirals into a massive and unfruitful conflict. I have just as often seen people overcome this kind of demonic influence by taking a break and clearing their heads or pausing to take a moment to remind those they are arguing with that they care about them. It usually doesn't take much to get out of this kind of influence. It is when we let this influence drive us that we run into problems.

So even though I had never before seen a demon affect the way an angel looked, I had often seen it between two people. And it makes sense that not only does the demonic want us to have an inaccurate view of other people; it wants us to have an inaccurate view of God and His purposes for us. It seemed that in this case the demon was trying to warp this man's view of justice, even God's justice.

Though the judge seemed to be doing his best to be reasonable, the man continued to argue until his fine was nearly doubled, a consequence of his continued belligerence. His face moving past crimson into shades of purple, he accepted the new paper handed to him by the bailiff, stomped past the police officers, and continued into the next room to pay his fine. His angel jogged to keep up with the man's brisk pace, a look of compassionate sadness on his face.

~

The judge shook his head as the man left, letting out a deep sigh and whispering something to the staff member on his left. After consulting a new stack of papers that had been set before him, he called out a name, and the man who gave up his seat to the elderly woman stepped up to the stand.

The judge outlined the terms of his case—something to do with an illegally parked car that was towed and impounded. As the judge spoke, I saw the demon with the thin wings begin to stretch and shiver as if it were trying to flex its muscles. I could still see the distorted image when I looked through the demon's wings. The same shadowy thoughts that were tormenting the man earlier began to reappear. Even more showed up this time, six or seven at once. They began to move and swirl into a thickening mass around the man's head. They spun faster and faster, coming in tighter and tighter around his face, neck, and eyes. Then the man's angel placed a firm hand on his shoulder. Instantly all the dark thoughts dissipated into vapor.

A look of frustration cut across the demon's face. It had been floating in midair, wings outstretched to each side, but when I looked again, it was beginning to sink down toward the ground. It started flapping its wings in an effort to remain airborne because the force that allowed it to remain aloft without effort was gone. The flapping made it much harder to see through the filter of its wings. Soon it gave up and slumped to the ground in an exhausted heap.

The man pleaded his case in a gentle, but sincere, manner. He had been out of work for some time, unable to repair his broken car and therefore unable to move it from where it was illegally parked. He had just gotten a new job and was working on getting together the money to get the car fixed, both to get it moved from where it was and to use it as a reliable means of transportation to his new job. But he and his family were already struggling to catch up from the time he had been out of work. The ticket and fees associated with getting the car out of impoundment were making the problem even worse. He did not beg. He did not demand. He just asked if there was a way for the judge to make it a little easier.

The judge canceled all fees associated with the case but told the man that, despite the problems he had been experiencing, he needed to be sure not to create a situation like this again.

The man walked out of the room to have his paperwork stamped and his fees waived. His angel followed close behind as he went, a broad grin stretched across his face.

I do not think the legal system is perfect. I do not think the courthouse I was visiting was a perfect example of heaven's justice. I do not think the judge was perfect, but I do think he was trying his best to be just. It might be easy to think an angel of justice as large and as powerful as the one I saw in the courtroom would be akin to a kind of blanket approval of everything and everyone operating there. However, I cannot think of a single perfect organization, business, school, or church, and yet I regularly see angels at all these places—sometimes angels carrying such authority and power that it makes my knees shake.

This angel of justice being present in the courtroom behind the judge was not a mark of unconditional support for what happened there—it was heaven partnering with man's attempt at creating justice on the earth. This is an important distinction. People often ask me what their angels are doing when they make poor decisions or when bad things are happening to them. The question is often presented in a "Why don't they do something about it?" sort of way. While I cannot claim to understand the exact nature of how heaven responds to every situation, experience has taught me that heaven has an answer for every problem that exists on earth, and that answer is present at ground zero of every one of those problems.

The justice of heaven was present for every single case that came before the judge that day while I was there. Do I think that perfect justice happened with each case? No. Would I have known how to dole out heaven's perfect justice in each of the cases I saw that day at the municipal court? Definitely not. I don't know exactly what perfect justice would have looked like with the belligerent man who yelled at the judge. Did he deserve to get his fines doubled because he was being mean and rude? Maybe. Would it have been heaven's justice to wipe away the fees of the rude man the same way the judge did with the sincere man? I am not really sure.

What I do know is this: heaven has an answer for every problem we face. If we want to learn how to see and hear what those answers are, then we need to start by learning how to see the world the way God does. I may not know what perfect justice should have looked like in those two particular cases I saw that day, but I bet there would have been a much better chance of both of those men receiving perfect justice if both of them had listened to what heaven was saying.

As a side note, the judge was kind enough to cut my penalties for driving without a valid tag in half. That was pretty reasonable, considering it was my procrastination that led to my not finding a ride to my side job and it was my choice to drive a vehicle with an expired tag.

Thoughts to Ponder

- The spirit realm is vast and full of intricate details. There were several other things I saw in the spirit at the municipal court that I did not mention in this chapter. There were hundreds of other things happening in the spirit that never caught my attention. There are dozens and dozens of details about the things I did mention in this chapter that I did not specifically address—such as the ash-colored mask that the demon blowing on the paper was wearing, how the angel with the samurai sword was wearing woven gold robes with red stitched detailing, and how the angry man's flailing gestures often knocked back his angel's attempts to calm and comfort him. Why do you think there is so much happening in the spirit realm?

- What do you think the main differences were between the belligerent man and the soft-spoken man? Was it their character, their mood, or their history that most influenced their ability to be more resistant or less resistant to demonic influence?

- If there was an angel of justice present during the proceedings of a small-town municipal court, then what other places might angelic influence be present in? In what other ways might heaven already be prepared to release itself on earth?

PEANUT BUTTER AND JELLY, BALLET, AND SOCCER PRACTICE

I WAS TEACHING AT A conference in southern Canada a few years ago. After the second session a woman came up to me and asked for prayer, or, more accurately, her family brought her up to me and asked for her.

"You don't have to, of course," she said quickly, "but I would be very grateful. But you don't have to."

I smiled, put my hand on her shoulder, and started praying. I heard the Holy Spirit saying how grateful He was for her heart, how great a gift she had been to everyone around her, and how much He liked to spend time with her. I shared these things, describing them as clearly as I could, though it felt difficult to get my words to match the feeling of love I felt welling in my chest for this woman.

After I finished saying what I had to say, the woman looked up at me, let out a sigh, and said, "Oh, good."

"What does that mean?" I asked.

"Oh, it's just…" She paused for a moment and then said, "Sometimes I just feel like I haven't done enough for God, you know?"

The second she said that, I felt the love in my chest turn into a deep, stabbing pain. It was so sudden and severe that I strained to keep a straight face. It did not last long, but the feeling of sadness that followed lingered for several seconds.

It was not disapproval or disappointment—just sadness. As I felt the sadness, pictures began to flash through my mind. I saw the woman chasing small children around. I saw her changing diapers and working on homework. I saw her making peanut butter and jelly sandwiches five at a time and driving kids to ballet and soccer practice. I saw her being a wonderful mom to wonderful children.

I recognized what was happening. She did not understand how valuable she was in God's eyes, how God had chosen her before she was even able to do anything on His behalf, how great His love was for her. She knew all these things, of course—I could see that in her eyes—but she did not understand them. I knew the truth, and I knew what I needed to say, but I too did not understand it. I knew that being a mother is one of the most valuable things you can do for God. I knew that God's love was shining upon her regardless of whether she did anything for Him. But I did not understand these things well enough to make them come out of my mouth. I could feel the feeble nature of my response brewing in my belly. I could hear how hollow "Of course you've done enough for God" or "God loved you since before the foundation of the earth" would sound, even though I believed those things were true. I could tell her how much it hurt the heart of God for her to say that, but it would almost certainly make her feel even worse. I could feel the sadness God felt at the idea of her feeling as though she had not done enough for Him. There was nothing condemning about it whatsoever; it simply mattered that much to Him that she knew how valued she was.

The pause in our conversation had already gone on too

long, so I gave up trying to find the right way to say what I was feeling. I loaded up the least cheesy and least hollow cliché I could manage, opened my mouth, and was cut off as her angel turned to look at me.

I had seen her angel there, of course, but I had not paid much attention until now. She had ivory skin and was tall and elegantly dressed. She also had a look of complete contentment and peace on her face. She looked me in the eye, let out a satisfied sigh, and said, "I am so grateful to have been assigned to her." She smiled and continued, "In being partnered with her, I have been able to be everything that the Father created me to be."

I froze for a moment, so touched by the affection I saw in the angel's eyes that I could not immediately bring myself to repeat what she had said. The woman was just as speechless when I finally shared it, but she quickly recovered and thanked me before departing with a huge smile on her face.

As I walked away from the conversation, I began to think about how hard it had been for me to find the words to express the love of God that I had felt pointed toward the woman. How could something I felt so clearly be so very difficult to express? The angel had found a way to express exactly what I was feeling using less than a tenth of the words I would have needed to describe it poorly. Her angel was able to reveal a facet of God's goodness that I wouldn't have been able to on my own.

I used to wonder why God bothered to create angels. Sure, I was grateful for them. I had seen them do hundreds of wonderful things, but when it came down to it, I couldn't figure out why they were necessary. God is God. He is omnipresent, omnipotent, and omniscient. He is everywhere, all powerful, and all knowing. Through the sacrifice of Jesus anyone can have a direct relationship with God. Why would we need angels in a situation like that?

I got the first part of the answer to this question one day while I was doing the dishes. The Holy Spirit suddenly asked me a question: "If you had more money than you would ever need, if every person in the world was saved, and if every person knew exactly how much God loved them, what would you do with your day-to-day life?"

I racked my brain, scrambling to come up with the right answer. Hundreds of possible answers, ranging from very cheesy to extremely dumb, flitted through my mind but nothing that felt close to right. Feeling as if I were taking way too long, I snatched up one of the cheesy ones: "I would, uh... find a way to serve You, Lord."

The Holy Spirit waited a few minutes before responding, possibly to let me think about how very lame my answer was, and then said, "Is what you do in your day-to-day life guided by need or by your relationship with Me?"

I set down the dish I was cleaning, turned off the water, and sat down on the couch. I sat there for several minutes, feeling stunned as I realized that so much of my perspective of my relationship with God was somehow tied to a need.

I need to accomplish great things for God. I need to teach people about God. I need to serve God. I need to follow God's plan. I need to grow in God. I need to grow a church that follows God's perfect structure.

I didn't think these were necessarily bad needs, but something about what the Holy Spirit said made the sense of urgency I felt behind those needs seem a little off base. I was suddenly overwhelmed with the reality that when it came down to it, God didn't need me at all. There was nothing I could accomplish that He could not do better and in less time. There was no lack in Him that I fulfilled. God did not need me at all. The only conclusion I could come to was this: God does not need me—God *wants* me.

If we look at our relationship with God through the lens of need, then we will distort and recolor every part of our interaction with Him. Relationships based on need are not relationships—they are alliances. They are mutually beneficial business deals. They are not bad, but they are less than what God is looking for with His children.

If we relate to God through need, then we will only talk to Him when we need something or just often enough that it doesn't feel awkward when we ask Him for something. Our salvation becomes nothing but a ticket into heaven rather than permission to have an intimate relationship with the Creator of the universe.

If we see the way God relates to us through the lens of need, then we are always trying to figure out what God wants us to do. We see God's plan for us as a set of marching orders that must be followed without error rather than the excitement of a Father who sees so much potential in His beloved child. We see sin as a long list of things we would probably like to do but cannot because they are "against the rules" rather than actions and thought patterns that violate the intimacy available between the Father and us. If we view worship through the lens of need, then it becomes an act of indulgence to a narcissistic and insecure deity rather than an expression of intimacy and love for a Father who is intimate and loving.

When we view angels through the lens of need, then it is easy to wonder what purpose they serve. As I mentioned previously, God is certainly powerful enough to accomplish anything an angel or an army of angels could. So what is the point of these celestial servants? Why do we need them at all?

If instead we view angels through the lens of a God who loves us and wants us, we begin to see their purpose shine through clearly.

Every person I have ever met has a personal angel. These angels follow us everywhere we go. They pray for us, worship with us, guard us, and partner with the plans of heaven for our lives. For whatever reason these angels spark that old question more than any other: What is the point of angels?

Maybe it is simply because personal angels, for lack of a better term, seem like such a luxury. Why would every single person on the planet need his or her own personal celestial attendant? After all, God is present and involved in every part of our lives, so what extra benefit could a personal angel possibly provide? It's not that I'm not grateful, but having a personal angel just seems a bit excessive, even redundant.

I found out why God chose to provide personal angels for everyone on the planet and discovered a huge piece of the purpose behind all angels shortly after my first son was born.

April and I had been married for just over a year. We had been talking about kids since before we were married, but this was the first time we really talked about making plans to start trying. The moment we agreed we were ready to start a family, an angel stepped into the room. It was of medium height, with brown hair and pleasant blue eyes, and wearing a nurse's uniform that looked as if it belonged on the set of a World War II movie. The angel followed April constantly for the three months we spent trying to get pregnant. It followed April once she was pregnant and continued following her as her pregnancy progressed. I would often see the nurse angel rubbing April's growing belly with a soft cloth, running fingers through her hair as she endured the discomfort of morning sickness, or massaging her back as the weight of our growing son began to strain her muscles.

It is common for a special angel to show up in a season of need or during a unique time in a person's life. I would often see an additional angel or two when someone was in a season of grief over the loss of a family member, when someone was learning to cope with the additional responsibility of a large promotion or new business venture, when young adults moved out of the house for the first time, and during many other seasons of great challenge or change. So I was not surprised that heaven would send a pregnancy angel to help us during this season. April and I needed all the help we could get.

The pregnancy angel continued to follow April all the way up to the day my son was born. It rode with us on the drive to the hospital while I drove ninety-five miles an hour to make it to the hospital in time. It was with us throughout her labor while my emotions oscillated wildly between excited, terrified, elated, and helpless. And it was with us in that indescribably powerful moment as April held Haydon for the first time.

After relishing the moment for as long as the medical staff would allow, I followed Haydon as he was taken to the examination table and the nurses tended to April. As I stood there, staring at that messy, wrinkly, and impossibly beautiful little face, I suddenly realized the pregnancy angel was standing next to me. It was staring at the brand-new baby boy just as intently as I was.

The pregnancy angel followed me as I escorted Haydon to another room for some tests. It stood right next to the little crib as I changed his diaper for the first time. It followed Haydon, never letting more than a step or two of space come between them, for the rest of the day.

Later that night—after all the bustle of visiting uncles, aunts, grandparents, and friends had subsided—April lay in the hospital bed fast asleep while Haydon slept soundly in the tiny hospital crib. The futon I was sleeping on seemed specially designed to cause lasting back problems, so despite being utterly exhausted, I was having a hard time falling asleep.

I kept staring at my sleeping son, feeling a love like none I had ever experienced well up in my chest with every passing second. Though it felt as if my eyes could not take enough of him in at once, I couldn't help but let my gaze repeatedly drift up to the angel as it stood on the opposite side of Haydon's crib. It was looking down at him with absolute affection. I recognized the look. It perfectly reflected the same overwhelming love I was feeling. I am sure the angel's expression matched my own. It was the one I had when I looked at my newborn son. It was the one I had when I looked at April. It was the look of love, the kind of love that can only happen between those who belong together.

"You're not a pregnancy angel," I said, looking up to meet the angel's eyes. "You're his angel, aren't you?"

The angel looked up to meet my gaze, smiled, and then nodded.

I could feel a heat rising in my chest. With it came a question I had asked in fits and starts for several years. What is the point of angels? What is the point of a personal angel?

Haydon's angel looked at me, smiled again, and then said, "What's wrong with the idea that the Father saw fit to send someone to love you every day that you are here on this earth?"

Personal angels do a lot of things for us. They pray for us, guard us, and support us—but these things are not their purpose. Personal angels exist because God wanted every person on this planet to have someone whose sole purpose was to love him or her well. Everything they do is an expression of this.

I have four children now, and I can tell you that each one of their angels showed up the moment April and I decided it was time to start trying to have a new baby. Each one followed April in the months we tried to get pregnant, throughout her pregnancy, and during every step of her labor, and then left to follow our newborn baby.

If we look through the lens of need, then we tend to look for function first and purpose second. We want to know what angels do and what we are supposed to do. But if we look through the lens of love, then we realize the first purpose of everything we see in the spirit is to be an expression of the love and kindness of our heavenly Father and that everything we do is meant to have its origins in that same love.

God is love. We are told this in 1 John 4:8. If we want to see in the spirit and understand the things we see, then we must learn to see everything through the lens of love. These are not rose-tinted glasses. This is not me advocating hyper-positivity. God's love is real. It is not so cheap as to sweep pain and suffering under the rug. But His love is good. It is profoundly good. To have the chance to discover just how good it is, we must be willing to look through the lens of love. We must be willing to let His love be the first thing we look for. This is the best way to see how much of His love is surrounding us and is woven into every part of our daily lives.

Thoughts to Ponder

- Recall some of the stories found earlier in this book. How does your perspective on these stories and the events in them change when you begin to practice viewing them through a lens of love?

- Learning to view things through a lens of love is a lifelong process. Take some time alone with the Lord and ask Him to show you where and how to begin adjusting your lens. We all have cracks and warps in different parts of our lens, but here are a few questions that may help get you started:

    1. How do I measure whether I am succeeding or failing?

    2. Do I feel close and connected to God or distant?

    3. What makes me feel close to Him when I am close?

    4. What makes me feel disconnected from Him when I am disconnected?

ACTIVATION AND STUDY— PURSUIT

FROM THE MOMENT I DISCOVERED seeing in the spirit was a gift, I was convinced it was a gift meant to be available to every Christian. I did not have any biblical or theological basis for this opinion, at least not at first; it was just a feeling, an innate belief that came along with the understanding that the things I saw were the result of a gift from God. Because of this belief, I was always happy to lay hands on people to try to impart the gift of seeing in the spirit. Between the ages of twelve and twenty-two I prayed for over three hundred people to receive the gift. Out of those three hundred only two received it—two people immediately and fully started seeing in the spirit with their physical eyes the moment I laid hands on them, but every other attempt at impartation showed not even the faintest spark of breakthrough.

Despite a success rate of less than 1 percent, my conviction that this gift was meant to be freely available for every Christian remained unshaken. I saw hundreds of angels on a weekly basis. Every person I met had an entire ecosystem of spiritual activity around him or her. Everywhere I went, something was happening in the spirit—layers of things were happening. The idea that God would create such a vibrant and robust spiritual reality but only give a small handful of people the ability to see it did not make any practical sense, and more importantly, it did not fit with His nature as a generous Father.

Even though my conviction refused to die, my results also refused to improve. I could not escape the thought that I was missing something important. Was I not laying my hands on people the right way? Was it not time for this gift to be shared? As someone who could see in the spirit from the time I was born, was I ill-equipped to teach others how to do it? Did the people I prayed for lack faith or character or some other essential trait? I could not find any answers, and I wasn't sure if I was even asking the right questions. Finally, after seven years of numerous failures and minimal success, I found the right questions.

I went to attend the Bethel School of Supernatural Ministry in Redding, California, when I was nineteen. There I began to learn about a spiritual gift I had never experienced myself: healing. The people at my previous church believed in healing; we even had a few testimonies of people being healed, but they were few and far between, and I had never seen anyone I prayed for be healed. I knew Bethel had a reputation for seeing numerous supernatural physical healings, and I was curious to see what the people there did to get results so dramatically different from the ones I saw growing up. It did not take me long to recognize the secret to their success. After only a few weeks I began to see two key differences between the way I had been praying for the sick and the way people prayed for the sick at Bethel.

First, they prayed for people constantly. I probably

prayed for ten people to receive healing before I came to Bethel. By the end of my first semester at the school of ministry, I prayed for well over a hundred. Many of the leaders at Bethel shared stories of praying for hundreds of people before seeing their first healing—although for many of them healings became more and more common in their lives after seeing that first miracle.

Second, they stewarded each healing. When I used to pray for people to be healed, I would lay my hands on them, pray, and then ask them if they felt better. Then they would say no or something polite but untrue, such as, "I think I might feel a bit better." Then I would shuffle away, feeling embarrassed. At Bethel they taught us to pray multiple times, ask people if they felt anything like heat or a tingling sensation, have them carefully test out the injury, if possible, and ensure they felt no pressure to say something was better if it wasn't. They taught that sometimes healing was a process of discovery. Jesus rarely performed healing the same way more than once. He even prayed for a blind man twice before his sight fully returned.

These two changes in style dramatically changed my personal experience with healing. Within a few months I went from having never once participated in a healing to seeing multiple people healed when I prayed. It did not take long for me to realize the principles I was learning about healing could also apply to the way I tried to impart the gift of seeing in the spirit.

My attempts to impart my gift usually went about as well as my attempts to release healing used to go. I laid my hands on them, prayed a simple prayer, and then asked them if they saw anything. The answer was the same more than 99 percent of the time: no.

Yet in the spirit I watched all the people I prayed for receive the gift of seeing in the spirit. Usually a small opening appeared above them with bright light shining through as a thin stream of golden oil poured out of the opening onto the tops of their heads and ran down their faces and into their eyes. Every person received the impartation, but almost no one walked away seeing in the spirit. After each prayer I would ask if they were seeing anything. When they said no, I would shrug my shoulders, smile awkwardly, and say something silly like, "Keep your eyes open, I guess," not knowing what else to do. People either saw in the spirit, or they didn't—what else was there to do?

After my first year at the Bethel School of Supernatural Ministry, I knew why no one was experiencing the gift I saw them receiving: I was imparting the gift of seeing in the spirit, but I was not teaching people how to steward and pursue the gift of seeing in the spirit. But how could people steward and pursue seeing in the spirit if they were not seeing anything? I was pondering this question one day when it hit me: even if people cannot see in the spirit yet, why couldn't the Holy Spirit just tell them what is happening around them?

I knew of many ministries that trained people to hear God's voice and operate in prophetic ministry. If God could tell people about His plans and people's hearts, then why would it be any harder for Him to tell people about what was happening in the spirit?

The first time I led a group of people through this

exercise—receiving a prophetic word about what is happening in the spirit—80 percent of the people in the room described something in the spirit that I was seeing with my eyes. They saw these things in their mind's eye or as an impression rather than with their physical eyes, but that did not change how shocked I was at their incredible accuracy.

I continued sharing this simple exercise whenever I got the chance, inspired by the shocking consistency with which people would hear, sense, or feel the same things I could see. As people continued to practice this exercise again and again, it wasn't long before some of them began seeing in the spirit with their eyes. After years and years of almost no success at sharing the gift God had given me, seeing in the spirit was finally growing in others, and it was growing fast.

Gifts of the Spirit

It has been twelve years since I first started teaching people how to steward and pursue the gift of seeing in the spirit. In that time I have seen more than enough evidence to further solidify the conviction I have always had: seeing in the spirit is a gift meant to be available for every Christian.

In this activation and study section I will be outlining a few of the keys I have discovered to unlocking the gift of seeing in the spirit in others. But before we delve deeper into how to see in the spirit, I want to take a moment to dispel a few misconceptions about how spiritual gifts work. I have run into a lot of mind-sets that hamstring people's ability to believe that seeing in the spirit and other gifts of the Spirit are available for them.

Misconception: Each person is only given certain spiritual gifts and does not receive others.

I constantly have people ask me questions such as "Can you see what spiritual gifts I have?" or "I think I might have the gift of prophecy. Can you see it on me?" While the gifts of the Spirit are indeed gifts since they can only come from God and we would be incapable of getting them on our own, the idea that we only have a few available to us reveals a supreme misunderstanding of God's generosity as a giver.

I believe every spiritual gift is available to every Christian. I also believe some of us have a natural talent for certain gifts in the same way some people are born with a natural talent for sports, mathematics, or painting. While it is true these natural bents will inform the amount of attention we tend to give certain gifts, I find it absurd that anyone would assume talent in one area should preclude us from talent in another. That is akin to saying being a gifted guitarist makes me unable to learn how to swim or severely limits my ability to become a swimmer.

Though it is true that some people find it much easier to learn how to see in the spirit than others, this does not mean the gift is meant for some and not for others—it just means we each have a unique journey of discovery for each of God's gifts. Many people who become great public speakers had a talent for speaking in public from a young age, and many others have stories of fighting through years of fear, doubt, and failure before becoming great public speakers. The speakers who were born with natural talent are not inherently better than the ones who were not; they just have a different story.

Some people use a passage in Romans 12 as evidence that each of us is only assigned one or a small handful of gifts.

> For by the grace given to me I say to everyone among you not to think of himself more highly than he ought to think, but to think with sober judgment, each according to the measure of faith that God has assigned. For as in one body we have many members, and the members do not all have the same function, so we, though many, are one body in Christ, and individually members one of another. Having gifts that differ according to the grace given to us, let us use them: if prophecy, in proportion to our faith; if service, in our serving; the one who teaches, in his teaching; the one who exhorts, in his exhortation; the one who contributes, in generosity; the one who leads, with zeal; the one who does acts of mercy, with cheerfulness.
>
> —ROMANS 12:3–8, ESV

I can see why people read these verses with this lens, but why then would we be encouraged to eagerly desire the spiritual gifts in 1 Corinthians?

> Pursue love, and earnestly desire the spiritual gifts, especially that you may prophesy.
>
> —1 CORINTHIANS 14:1, ESV

We are even encouraged to chase after one gift in particular: prophecy. Why would we be asked to pursue a specific gift if only certain people are meant to receive that gift?

I do not think that Romans 12 is saying that only certain people get certain gifts. I believe it is asking us to recognize that no one gift is inherently more valuable than another, that each of us will express these gifts in a different way according to the measure of faith God has assigned, and that the different ways these gifts are expressed through us are not inherently more valuable than any other way they are expressed.

You may not be born with the talent or physical makeup to be a world-class race car driver, but that does not mean you shouldn't even bother learning how to drive. Think of all the freedom, joy, and opportunity you would miss out on if you believed this way. Seeing in the spirit may not be one of the main gifts you are called to carry, but that does not mean you do not have access to all of the revelation, clarity, and peace that can come from it.

Do not underestimate the generosity of our heavenly Father.

Misconception: Certain special people receive certain special spiritual gifts that are not meant for everyone.

Sometimes people ask me, "Blake, you can see in the spirit all the time. You were born with this gift. Don't you think that God just decided to give you a special gift for a specific purpose? How can you believe everyone has access to what you have?"

While I agree that God does divinely give specific people special gifts, this question comes from a misunderstanding about why God does this. I believe God gives outstanding gifts to certain people as a marker of the standard of what is available to all His children.

People with an amazing evangelistic gift are not just called to lead thousands of people to the Lord—they are called to show what it looks like to be empowered by God to lead people to the Lord. People with an outstanding prophetic gift are not just called to give impactful words of direction and encouragement to people—they are called to reveal the kind of conversation life available to all who are in relationship with God. People with an exceptional gift of joy are not just called to release joy on people—they are called to be an example of the joy meant to be the standard of life with God.

The Bible is full of examples of this principle, but I can think of none clearer than the life of Jesus. The word Christ means anointed one. If there is one example of someone who had a special gift meant only for him, then surely the Son of God is that example, right? Jesus did not just go around performing miracles so people would know who He was—He equipped His disciples to do the same. In fact, He told them they would do even greater things than He did (John 14:12). Not only was Jesus meant to be the source of salvation; He is also the example of what life in relationship with God looks like, a standard we are invited to pursue.

I do believe I have divinely received a special gift; I just also believe I am no more special than anyone hand-crafted by the King of all kings. We are all intended to excel well beyond the norm in the areas God has called us to. We are also meant to receive the benefit of one another's excellence. In this way a finite people can begin to reveal the nature of an infinite God.

Misconception: Because these gifts are divinely given, I should divinely know how to use them.

People sometimes get the idea that the gifts of the Spirit should come with inherent knowledge of how and when to use them. This is not the case. There are dozens of examples in this book as well as in my previous book, *The Veil*, of how I have struggled to learn how to use this gift even though I was born with it.

God loves process. He designed life to grow. Moses spent forty years being prepared to lead his people out of Egypt. Elisha spent around eight years serving under Elijah before he picked up the prophetic mantle and became prophet in Elijah's place. There were fifteen to twenty years between when David was anointed as king and when he actually took the throne. Even Jesus spent thirty years growing in wisdom and stature before starting His public ministry.

As humans we have to learn how to do everything—it is how we were designed by the Creator. We have to learn to crawl, walk, and run. We have to learn how to talk, follow directions, and make friends.

Your hands are a gift from God. They can be used to write in a hundred languages, paint masterpieces, play beautiful music, throw a ball with incredible accuracy, and comfort a friend. Your hands had everything they needed to do all these things and more on the day you were born, yet at first you were only able to make your fingers into a fist. If you teach your hands, they can do any or all of the things I have listed. If you do not, then they cannot.

God has divinely bestowed upon all His children hundreds of spiritual and physical gifts. They are all there, waiting for you to learn how to use them. Though some do have a natural talent for certain specific gifts, even they need to learn how to unleash the full measure of that talent.

Misconception: Failure is a sign I do not have a particular gift.

Failure is an inherent part of learning. When my son was learning to walk, he fell dozens and dozens of times. It would have been foolish for me to conclude that my son's repeated failure to walk was a sign he probably just wasn't meant to walk. Between the ages of one and three, when my son was learning to talk, he pronounced about 10 percent of what he said correctly. It would have been foolish for me to tell my son that he should probably stop talking, that this clearly was not a gift God had for him, since he was confusing people with all those mispronounced words.

When people are learning to see in the spirit, they often ask, "What if I am just imagining these things? What if I get it wrong? What if I do not discern the meaning behind what I am seeing correctly?" My usual answers to these questions are that these people will probably imagine some of it, they will certainly get it wrong from time to time, and they are not going to accurately discern the meaning behind what they are seeing every time. However, if they do not get comfortable with the idea of failure so they can practice, then they will never be able to tell the difference between their imaginations and the voice of God, they will never have the opportunity to get it right, and they will never be able to discern the meaning behind what they see in the spirit.

My son was not good at walking when he first got started, so I did not take him to practice near the edge of a canyon or near a busy highway. I let him practice in my house, where I had removed the coffee table with sharp corners, put a thick carpet down on the hard floor, and left plenty of sturdy things for him to hold on to. I stayed in the room with him, helping him practice his balance, lifting him up when he fell, and celebrating with him when he succeeded.

I do not tell people to start their journey of pursuing the gift of seeing in the spirit by telling a stranger on the street what his personal angel looks like or by publicly announcing during a staff meeting that they are going to point out any demons in the room. I encourage people to find a small group of friends to practice with. I tell them to get started by looking in the spirit during a church service or at home while listening to worship music.

Recognizing that failure is part of learning equips us to learn from our failures and reminds us to create safe places for us to practice.

~

These are just a few of the common misconceptions about the gifts of the Spirit that I run into on a regular basis. As simple as many of them may seem, I have seen dozens and dozens of people sabotage their ability to see in the spirit, or operate in many other gifts, because they believe one of these falsehoods. The truth is simple: God wants you to see in the spirit because He wants you to see what He is doing. Seeing in the spirit, as with all the gifts of the Spirit, is a window into His nature, and the more we gaze upon His nature, the easier it becomes to adopt it as our own.

Steward and Pursue

Pursuing God is an exercise in balance. The fastest way to grow spiritually is to be completely satisfied with what He has given us while remaining desperately hungry for the promises we have yet to see fulfilled. If we lean too hard on being satisfied with what He already gave us, then we can easily slip into complacency, missing out on receiving the full inheritance Jesus won for us on the cross. If we become too desperate and focused on promises yet to be fulfilled, we can easily become jaded and disappointed, harming our connection with God and perhaps limiting our ability to experience the benefit of the gifts He gave us.

I do not let my son drive my car. This is not because I do not trust his judgment or character. He is a good learner, attentive, healthily cautious, and considerate. He has all the character traits I want to see in a quality driver. It is not because I think my car is too nice for him or too fast for him. I do not let my son drive my car because he is seven years old. It is not time for him to drive, not because of any lack in him whatsoever but because it is not the season for him to drive yet. He would not be a more fulfilled, significant, or important seven-year-old if I let him drive my car. No matter his merits, if I told you I was letting my seven-year-old drive me to work every day, you would probably call the police.

It is easy to imagine how if my son became fixated on driving and viewed it as a symbol of his value, his merit, or my love for him, that perspective could make his daily life quite painful. Every day when I hopped in the car and drove off somewhere, he would feel as if it were an insult. He would see the hundreds of people who drive around in cars every day and wonder what they had that he did not.

As obvious as this illustration may seem, it is important to understand that only our shared cultural perspective makes the idea of my seven-year-old resenting me for not letting him drive absurd. We have a cultural and legal system that tells us that seven is too young to drive.

My son has no real understanding of the cultural and legal norms that dictate when he is and is not old enough to drive. He only has trust in me when I tell him that it is not time yet. You and I can fully appreciate all the reasons he is not ready to drive. It is an issue of maturity—not that he is immature; he is in fact very mature and astute for a seven-year-old. Yet he lacks a kind of maturity that he could not, and probably should not, have at the age of seven. It is not wrong or bad; it is simply not time yet. I want my son to drive. I am excited for the day I get to climb in a car with him and begin to teach him. But I am also just as excited about all the wonderful things I get to teach and do with him on the way to that day.

I know I am driving this silly metaphor into the ground, but it is important. I have met so many people who have driven themselves mad trying to figure out what is keeping them from seeing in the spirit or some other spiritual gift. It breaks my heart to see people damage their connection with their heavenly Father over something that is as firmly and confidently laid out in the plan for their lives as my son's eventual ability to drive. I do not always know how long a path or what kind of maturing or what detail will lead to breakthrough, no more than a nine- or ten-year-old can truly understand the kind of maturity that my seven-year-old son will need to become a driver. The truth is, there is nothing my son could do to make his season of driving come sooner.

We need to trust that God sees more than we do, that He is looking forward to the day we inherit every bit of what His Son won for us on the cross, and that He is excited about every step of the journey to get there. I am not saying we cannot do anything to undermine our ability to operate in the gifts of the Spirit. My son could certainly begin making choices and showing character traits that would make me question if he were ready to have a driver's license. I may even forbid him from taking his driver's test if these choices or traits became severe enough; however, I would not consider myself a very good father if I did not make it abundantly clear why this privilege was being taken away from him and how he could get it back.

God is faithful to lead us to every good thing He has for us. If there is something in the way, He will tell you. If there is nothing in your way, then maybe you are still on a journey; maybe you are exactly on the part of the journey you are supposed to be on.

So then what do you do in the meantime? To take my little metaphor a step further, what if my seven-year-old son was exceedingly excited about the day he gets to drive a car? What if he dreamed every day about being a race car driver? What if becoming a great driver was one of his

highest aspirations? Well, being a good father, I would connect with him through this subject. I would buy him toy
cars of all sizes. I would let him play the highest-quality
racing video games. I would take him to car shows, teach
him about engines, let him work on the family car with me,
talk with him about driving, and dream with him about
driving. I would learn more about cars just so I would have
more to teach him. And God is a much better father than
I am.

The following is an exercise I have taught for over twelve
years. It is not a patented three-step method, guaranteed to
make you a bona fide seer in three weeks or less. It is a
way to connect with your Father on the subject of seeing
in the spirit. It is a way to play with toy cars and work on
the family car as you dream about the day you get to drive.
As I said before, it will not automatically make you a seer,
but it will prepare you for the day you begin to see and, in
the meantime, further connect you to the giver of all good
gifts.

Practice

I recommend, for at least your first few attempts, practicing during worship at a church service. A worship service is a great place to learn to see in the spirit. There are
many layers of things going on, it is easier to focus on
God's presence when others are doing the same, and many
of the things that happen in the spirit during a worship
service are very intuitive and easy to understand.

I usually try to find a place at the back of the room
where I have a nice wide view of the space. I start by

spending the first few minutes just engaging in worship. I want to make sure I am not just going through a routine but engaging with God and what He is doing in the room. Once I feel settled, here is the simple process I use to let the Lord lead me to what He wants to show me; it is the same exercise I use to teach people to pursue the gift of seeing in the spirit.

1. Close your eyes and ask the Holy Spirit where to look.

You may feel immediately drawn to a specific place, such as the front of the stage or behind one of the worship leaders. You might see a picture of a place in the room in your mind's eye. You may just feel a slight impression pulling you toward a general area. Typically when the Holy Spirit wants to show me something, I feel a gentle tugging sensation, as if my equilibrium is subtly tipping in a certain direction. The Lord speaks to us all differently, so He can lead you to look somewhere in any number of ways. Whatever you do, don't overthink it. If you cannot settle on exactly where you should be looking, then just pick a spot. This is one of the reasons I recommend a worship service as the first place to practice. You would be surprised how much is happening in the spirit every time we worship. You could really look almost anywhere. Remember, it is better to try and fail than to get stuck in the details.

2. Open your eyes, look at the spot, and ask the Holy Spirit to show you what is there.

Look for big things, and look for small things. I have had people instantly see in the spirit with their physical eyes on their first attempt. Some people see something big and dramatic; if that happens to you, then celebrate. Many people see smaller things, such as a ripple in the air, a brief flash or streak of light, or a blurry glowing outline; if you see any of these things, then celebrate. Many of the spiritual things I see clearly on a regular basis today only appeared as a vague outline or flash of light the first time I saw them. Oftentimes understanding leads to further clarity, but sometimes that clarity only comes after weeks or months of practice.

If you do not see anything with your physical eyes, then please do not lose heart. Ask the Holy Spirit to tell you what is happening where you are looking. You may see a picture in your mind's eye, feel an impression, or hear a brief description in a still, small voice. It may not feel as satisfying or significant to get an impression or picture of what is happening in the spirit, but this is where we get to exercise our ability to be satisfied with what God is doing now while we continue to pursue what He has promised.

A mature gift of seeing in the spirit requires a great deal of trust between you and God. We learn to develop that trust as we learn to hear His voice. Even if you are not seeing with your eyes yet, you are investing in a relationship that will be the foundation of every spiritual gift you operate in for the rest of your life.

3. Ask the Holy Spirit to explain what you are seeing.

This is a simple, but very important, part of the process. This is what will develop your understanding of how the spirit realm works, equipping you to make good use of the things you see and clearly discern their purpose. Ask the Holy Spirit tons of questions. Why is that angel standing that way? Why is it carrying a staff? Why is the staff made of gold? Why is it etched to look as if it is covered in leaves? You can still ask questions, even if you are not seeing a lot of detail. Why did that streak of light move from the roof to the ground rather than the other way around? Why is that blur of light swaying back and forth in time with the music? Why can I only see that angel out of the corner of my eye? You may not get answers to all your questions— you may not get answers to any of them—but you will exercise your ability to have a conversation with the Holy Spirit about what you are seeing.

I have led hundreds of people in this exercise and seen a massive variety of results. People have immediately seen full-blown open visions of angels carrying scrolls with handwritten messages from the Father on them, and other people have tried this exercise a dozen times with little or no results. People have seen angels for a moment, only to have the angels vanish the next moment. People have seen and sensed nothing, only to go home to find an angel standing in their bedroom.

The results from this exercise consistently vary widely during people's first few attempts. I have noticed, however, that as people continue this exercise, practicing it at home, at church, during their commute, and in any other place they have the mind to look, a pattern begins to emerge. They begin to see more with their eyes. It becomes easier to have conversations with the Holy Spirit about the things they see. And before long seeing starts to become a more normal part of their lives.

No two people's journeys have been the same. I met

a girl who diligently pursued this gift for a week, doing this exercise four times a day, and then started seeing in the spirit with her physical eyes by the end of the week. I know a man who did this exercise multiple times a week—checking what he was sensing with me to see if I was seeing what he was feeling whenever he had the chance—for three years. After three years of persistent pursuit he suddenly began seeing in the spirit with his physical eyes.

I do not know how long or how hard you will pursue this gift before you experience it, but I do know that for all the people I know who have received it, the journey has been just as valuable as the destination because it is a journey that you get to take with your Father.

Additional Practice

As I said previously, I recommend practicing during a worship service for the first several times. It is a safe place where it is easy to focus on what God is doing, and there are a wide variety of things that happen in worship. However, if you continue to pursue this gift, then I am sure you will soon be hungry for more variety in your practice sessions, so here are a few more activations and practice ideas that I have done over the years.

You can apply the same basic technique I have outlined, but remember that this is more about you learning to cooperate with the Holy Spirit than following a formula. I've also included some questions to get you thinking and looking in the right direction. You may not be able to discern or see the answers to all these questions at first, but they will help guide your conversation with the Holy Spirit.

Prayer

Go to a prayer meeting, or host one at your home. Practice seeing what is happening in the spirit while people pray. What kinds of things are released as they pray? How do these things change as the tone and focus of the prayer shift? How do things look different in the spirit when one person is praying as opposed to another? How does it look when individuals are praying versus when a whole group is praying together?

Bible study

Go to a Bible study, or host one at your home. Look to see what happens in the spirit when people study the Bible together, read it quietly to themselves, or share with one another what they have learned. How does the spiritual activity in the room change as people shift from casual conversation to the study of the Bible? What is happening in the spirit around a person as he or she reads the Bible silently? What is happening in the spirit when someone is reading a passage aloud? How does the spiritual atmosphere shift and change as people discuss a particular passage? How do the angels respond when Scripture is read?

Personal angels

This can be a good way to practice in a group as well as on your own. Simply try to look for an individual's personal angel. Where is the person's angel standing in relation to him or her? What color clothing is the angel wearing? What is the angel's demeanor (e.g., solemn, energetic, peaceful, joyful, friendly)? What is the angel doing?

Church/house

Churches and homes often have angels that consistently remain in the same place or move in a consistent route through the area. Go from room to room looking for any angels that are present as well as any other spiritual structures. Is there a part of the building that has more spiritual activity than other parts? What kinds of angels are you finding (e.g., worship angels, protection angels, angels carrying healing)? How does the spiritual atmosphere shift as you move from room to room?

~

These are all, of course, just suggestions. You could just as easily practice seeing in the spirit at a public library, at your dentist's office, at the grocery store, or on the freeway during a traffic jam, but the locations listed here are some of the best places to start.

The last thing I want to emphasize once more is the value of finding a group to practice with or, at the very least, a good and grounded friend to give you honest feedback about your thoughts and experiences. Every spiritual gift is meant to work within the context of community and healthy relationships, and it is our personal responsibility to identify and integrate ourselves into a healthy spiritual community.

This is one of the reasons that I have spent the last ten years of my life serving at a school of ministry much like the one I attended when I was nineteen. My life was completely transformed by the growth I experienced there. There is an acceleration that happens when people from all over the world come together to dedicate a season of their lives to the pursuit of identity in Christ and the perpetuation of His kingdom. I have never felt anything else quite like it.

You don't have to go to a school like the Bethel Atlanta School of Supernatural Ministry to find this kind of environment, of course; all you have to do is find people who are hungry and chase after His kingdom together. Whether it looks like joining a school of ministry, attending a prophetic class, or starting a weekly worship night with a group of friends, find people to run with. You need them, and they need you.

I WALKED INTO THE BACK of the church feeling frustrated and defeated. I had decided for the third and final time that I was never talking about seeing in the spirit ever again. There was just no way to get anything good out of it. When I told people about the angels I saw, they asked me a hundred questions I couldn't answer. When I told people about the demons I saw, they got angry or scared. Half the things I saw were too abstract or unclear to be useful. The other half were clear in that I could see and describe them in a reasonably normal way, but I only understood bits and pieces of why those things were there and what they were doing.

I slumped down into my usual spot in the back row with my arms crossed and a scowl on my face. A mass of liquid light was slowly oscillating above the stage as the worship team played a gentle melody. It was bluish green in parts, reddish yellow in others, and purplish orange in the middle.

"Great," I thought, "here is another abstract, confusing, and useless spiritual thing, another thing I don't understand, another thing I don't know how to describe."

I already gave up sharing the things I saw twice before, convinced they brought more confusion than wisdom. And twice I felt guilty after a few months, certain that if God gave me this gift, He wanted me to use it to benefit other people. But no matter how hard I tried, I struggled to share the things I saw with clarity and to pull any meaningful value from them. Sure, people were encouraged when I told them angels were dancing while they were leading worship, and people seemed to feel a bit more secure when I described what kind of angel was watching over them, but that was it.

The most frustrating part was that none of what I saw felt confusing when I saw it. Even if I did not understand its nature or purpose, I felt that there was a nature and purpose behind each thing. Whenever I tried to explain that feeling, however, my words almost always fell flat and lifeless to the ground, carrying none of the beauty and vitality I felt when I saw those things.

Even as I watched the bluish, reddish, purplish blob of light above the stage, I did not understand it, but some part of my soul found it deeply familiar. As I concentrated on that feeling, my eyes were suddenly drawn to an elderly woman sitting in the front row. She was hunched all the way over so that her face and folded hands were pointed toward the ground as she rocked gently back and forth to the sound of the music.

Then a thought appeared—not from the front of my mind but from somewhere at the back. My church had a wonderful and wide variety of worship leaders. Because of this, worship was one of the things my church was famous for. Because of this strength a mind-set had begun to develop in the culture of the church. It wasn't anything that anyone said directly, just a belief system that developed in the general group consciousness. If I were to put words to this mind-set, they would be something like: real worshippers dance, sing loudly, or at least raise their hands.

So as I looked at the woman sitting hunched over, the thought at the back of my mind was "I guess she is not really engaged in worshipping God," although it never manifested as anything as clear as that. It was more of a feeling. The second this feeling took root in my mind, however, conviction twisted at the muscles in my chest.

I looked closer at the woman, and as I did, I saw straight through her. I could see every bone and every organ in shimmery, translucent layers, similar to an X-ray. Tilting my head and leaning back and forth let me see different parts—rib cage, lungs, liver. Then something caught my eye as her heart came into focus. A little blob of light was oscillating through the four chambers of her heart, flowing in perfect rhythm with every heartbeat. I realized as I looked closer that it was a bluish, reddish, purplish blob of light.

My eyes snapped back up to the area above the stage where a perfect, yet oversized, replica of the light in the woman's heart moved back and forth in the exact same pattern and rhythm. I looked around the room and found an exact copy of the pattern of light and color in the heart of each and every person in the room. Then the Holy Spirit spoke to me in a crystal clear voice: "I am syncing their heartbeats to Mine."

I felt guilty for judging the woman, of course, but that feeling felt small in comparison with the understanding of God's kindness and presentness that came from seeing how He was leading His people into a deeper encounter with Him. I sat through the rest of the worship service with a big smile on my face. It felt surprisingly satisfying to see something so elusive and abstract be suddenly and completely filled with so much meaning. I thought about all the moments of frustration and confusion that came when I tried to share the things I saw with other people. Maybe I was supposed to share the things I saw with other people, but I just couldn't. No matter how hard I tried, I couldn't seem to imbue my words with the joy, comfort, and revelation that came from everything I saw. Even if I tried to share about something as simple and peaceful as the gently moving light above the stage and how it was affecting the heart of everyone in the room, I knew that none of the peace I felt would make the transfer from sight to words.

I made my decision, this time from a place of determination rather than frustration. I was not going to talk about seeing in the spirit anymore. I could not, in good conscience, share what I saw if the goodness, peace, and love I felt when I saw it could not be included in the transaction.

PART II

God in Heaven

GOD IS EVERYWHERE. HIS HAND touches everything. Nowhere and no one is outside His reach. He has a perfect plan for everyone and everything. He has hopes and dreams for us that are leaps and bounds beyond our wildest dreams.

So then how do I—a normal person with needs and ambitions of my own, a family to love and care for, and plenty of bills to pay—pursue the plans and purposes of God? How do I know I am going in the right direction? How can I possibly have any meaningful effect in plans so big and far-reaching? How does God's perfect plan respond to my hurts and pains?

In the following section you will find stories about some of the ways God reveals who He is to us, how He invites us into His purposes on the earth, and how we can begin the journey of seeing all God's hopes and dreams come to pass. Look for how God's intentions are revealed through His actions and how you can develop a new lens for viewing your life and your potential.

WOUNDS

ONE DAY MY WIFE, APRIL, and I were in an argument. We were not arguing about anything serious, and neither of us was especially angry; we just weren't seeing eye to eye.

As our discussion wore on, a sentence popped into my head. I knew right away it was not the right thing to say. It wasn't anything horrible, of course, but it was neither productive nor kind. I knew this, but as our conversation continued to go in repetitive circles, someplace in the back of my brain was insisting that, despite its unkind nature, it would feel really satisfying to say it. So before my better nature could get the best of me, I threw out the statement that had been knocking around in my mind.

Immediately I saw a small cut appear on my wife's cheek. It was small, only about two inches long, but deep enough to draw a single drop of blood.

"Shoot," I said, feeling shocked.

"What?" April asked, thrown off by my sudden change in tone.

"I shouldn't have said that."

"Oh, it's fine," she said, waving a hand.

"No," I insisted, watching the drop of blood run down the side of her cheek, "it was not fine. I should not have said that, and I am very sorry that I did."

She smiled and said, "It's OK. I forgive you."

The drop of blood ran back up her cheek as the cut sealed itself up, leaving no sign it had ever been there.

I see spiritual wounds on people everywhere I go. From minor lacerations, such as the one caused by my unkind words to my wife, to the deep and repeated gashes from lifelong trauma and abuse, wounds are an unavoidable factor of life on earth.

I see wounds on just about everyone I meet. They vary greatly in severity and quantity. Some appear swollen and infected, signs that bitterness and unforgiveness are beginning to take hold. Some look tended and clean, signs the person is letting God lead him or her into healing. Sometimes only scars remain, a sign that while the wound is no longer present, the memory of the pain the wound caused is still very much alive.

We all experience wounds, but we do not all experience them the same way. I have watched something simple, such as someone not saying hello when passing by in the hall, fester and grow into a wound so severe that it affected every single day of the wounded person's life. I have watched something severe, such as multiple affairs and a messy divorce, be completely transformed into a crown of glory by the wounded person's willingness to submit his or her wounds to the care of the Holy Spirit.

I do not know what God's answer is for every pain that exists in this world, but I have learned enough about the nature of His goodness to trust He has an answer for every single one of the pains. I am also familiar enough with my own nature to know that unless I am willing to run the risk of trusting He is as good as He says He is, then I will not see His goodness or how it responds to suffering.

~

When I was in college, I had two friends who were very similar. They were both about the same height, were the same age, had the same hair color, and even had the same first name. I will call one Jack and one John.

Jack and John also had very similar backgrounds. Both had fathers who were almost never present and who were physically and verbally abusive when they were. Both had mothers who were manipulative, controlling, and unstable. Both hardly spoke to anyone in their families anymore. Both had worked hard to overcome the wounds of their past.

Jack and John got married within a few years of each other, and both of their weddings were nearly ruined by violent outbursts from their broken families. Both Jack and John married young and had a hard time adjusting to married life. From this point on, however, Jack's and John's lives became very different.

Jack and his wife moved in with his wife's parents while he and his wife both finished getting their degrees. Jack was frequently overwhelmed by how overbearing his wife's parents were. They pushed their way into every conflict between Jack and his wife, always taking her side and vilifying him. He quickly started to shut down, avoiding conflicts whenever possible. There was no point in arguing when he was constantly outnumbered.

I watched new spiritual cuts and bruises appear on Jack

each time I saw him. Even though there was hardly any conflict in his marriage anymore, the suppressed emotions caused even more damage than the constant fighting had. Before long, Jack wouldn't even talk with me about the challenges in his marriage. He shut out everyone. Maybe he felt ashamed that his relationship was not going as well as the relationships he saw around him. Maybe he thought things would get better if he just changed himself to accommodate the expectations and needs of his wife and her family. I don't know; he didn't tell me. But I watched as the wounds across his face, arms, and neck grew more and more infected with every passing week.

John had a hard first year of marriage as well. The pain and chaos that marked his upbringing had given him no model of what healthy relationships look like. He would frequently overreact to small things his wife would say and do, even if no hurt was intended. Small misunderstandings would erupt into hours of conflict, exhausting John and his wife and stealing the joy from their relationship.

I watched new spiritual wounds appear on John almost every day, but I noticed something different about the wounds he received. Though his wounds were more numerous and often more severe than the ones I saw on Jack, John's wounds were disappearing as quickly as they were showing up. Every time I saw Jack, his infected cuts and bruises were accompanied by a few new lacerations. Every time I saw John, the old cuts were gone, replaced by new ones.

When I asked John about how he was doing, he said although things were still hard, he and his wife quickly sought out a counselor to help them. They each sought out mentors and spiritual mothers and fathers to speak encouragement and wisdom into their lives. After a few more months I realized I was seeing fewer and fewer wounds on John. In fact, I soon saw some of the scars left from the pain of his childhood begin to disappear.

Jack's and John's lives continued to diverge. Eventually Jack's pain led him into having an affair. The severity of the situation led Jack and his wife to spend a year focusing on fixing their crumbling marriage. They started getting counseling, and things did get better. But unfortunately I still see the old wounds of his childhood and the new wounds of his marriage affect every day of his life, even to this day.

John and his wife only continued to grow closer. They have three children. They work together in full-time ministry. They are not perfect. Challenges still arise, but I see them overcome those challenges, and I see the wounds that come from those challenges get healed again and again.

We all have different backgrounds. We all face different challenges. It can be easy to compare your history or your present challenges with someone else's and feel he or she has it easier. I can even look at my two friends' lives and pick out circumstances that made John's situation easier than Jack's. But I know that is not why John's life has only gotten better and Jack's has kept falling apart.

We cannot always control whether we receive spiritual wounds, but we can control how we respond to them. We can decide to protect ourselves from being hurt again—to keep people at a safe distance, suppress our needs, and avoid vulnerability—but this only sets us up for more pain.

Jack's childhood formed his view of the world. His

wounds taught him what to expect from people. Further wounds only reinforced these expectations and set him up for more wounds and more pain.

John's childhood formed his worldview too. But when that worldview started to cause pain in his new marriage, John looked for help. He found mentors. He found spiritual mothers and fathers. He found wise counselors. He found people to help reshape the lens created by his childhood. He spent time in the presence of God, letting the Lord give him a worldview marked by His profound good rather than wounds and pain.

We all get to choose how we respond to being wounded. We get to choose to hold on to our wounds and let them teach us how to see life, or we get to choose to give our wounds to God and let Him teach us how to see life. We may need help learning how to give it to God. That's OK. Whatever it takes, it is worth learning how to receive the healing God has for each of us. No matter how severe or unjust the wounds in your life are, God has a perfect plan for perfect restoration every single time.

Thoughts to Ponder

- How do you think wounds affect our perception of the world around us, both in the physical and in the spirit?

- Looking back, do you find yourself responding to pain more like Jack or more like John?

- How do you think God feels about the hurts and wounds we experience throughout life?

GOD AND PAIN

A FEW YEARS AGO I was speaking at a conference in eastern Texas. I had just finished a long question-and-answer session and was desperately looking for the nearest bathroom when a woman approached me with her hands folded neatly in front of her.

"Excuse me," she said in a quiet voice. "I have one more question, if that's all right."

"Sure thing," I said, looking over her shoulder to see if the bathroom was in that direction.

"Well, it's not a question exactly, I guess…" She rubbed her hands together as her gaze drifted back and forth between me and the floor. "How do you…How can I…"

I refocused my attention on her and realized she was holding back tears.

Taking in a deep breath, all at once she asked, "Could you just pray for my daughter?"

"Definitely," I answered. "Is she here today?"

"Yes. Well, no. Well, she'll be here later this afternoon." She bit her lip. "It's just been a hard time for our family, you know. We've always been a normal family. Normal, you know."

"I'd be happy to pray for her," I said, feeling very curious, but not wanting to cause any more distress. "Just grab me before the next session starts, and I'll pray for her."

"OK. Thank you," she said, and she walked off with tears forming in the corners of her eyes.

I continued in search of a bathroom, feeling a rising sense of foreboding at the back of my mind.

I have been sharing my gift publicly for ten years now, and in that time I have prayed for a lot of people for a lot of different reasons. Being in ministry tends to acquaint you with a very wide spectrum of human experience. I regularly meet people celebrating in the midst of their greatest victories, sifting through the pieces of their greatest failures, or facing the harsh reality of their greatest tragedies. Sometimes I encounter people in all three situations on the same day. Thankfully I learned quickly that I am not responsible for solving every problem presented to me. I am responsible for saying what God is saying and doing what God is doing.

Because of that I am rarely overwhelmed by the problems people are facing. I have been thrust into the middle of impossible and overwhelming situations many times before, and God always has something to say—to expect any less would be a disservice to my history with Him. Still, something about the quivering pain I saw behind the woman's eyes left a lingering dread I could not seem to shake.

Later that night I walked back into the main room where the conference was being held. The worship band was already playing. The woman I had spoken to was nowhere in sight, so I found a spot in the back of the room and waited. A few minutes later I felt a tap on my shoulder.

"So, my daughter said she is OK with you praying for her," the woman said, trying to talk quiet enough not to be overheard but loud enough that I could hear her over the music, "but she doesn't want to come into the sanctuary."

"OK," I said, feeling slightly confused.

"I talked her into coming into the foyer though."

"OK," I said, feeling slightly more confused.

"You see," she said as her voice cracked a little, "I just don't know how much to tell you."

I said, "A little bit of background would be helpful, I think."

"Well...uh, then..." She took in a sharp breath. "Can I tell you in the foyer? Then I'll go get her."

"OK," I said, and I followed her into the foyer.

"So earlier this year my daughter met this...young man," the woman said as the door to the sanctuary closed, muffling the sound from the worship band. "My husband and I didn't feel great about him, but he seemed nice enough."

She went on to tell me about how he kept buying expensive gifts for her daughter and taking her on elaborate dates, how her daughter had started sneaking out to spend more time with this guy, and how anytime she tried to talk to her daughter about how uncomfortable she felt about the relationship, her daughter would get mad or end the conversation abruptly.

She told me about how this man kidnapped her daughter and pulled her into the world of human trafficking. She told me about the anguish their family went through as the police searched for their lost daughter; how every day was a roller coaster of hope and disappointment, anger and sorrow; and how after three months the police were finally able to track down where her daughter had been taken and get her back.

She told me about how grateful they were to have her back, but as she did, some part of me could not help but think about how much bad could happen in three months.

"It's just been hard, you know," she said, wiping away tears. "We have her. She's back, but it's just not the same. I mean, how could it be? She's only fifteen." She cut herself off with another gush of tears.

My arms and legs felt numb. I had been completely silent as she recounted her story, unable to find an adequate response. My heart ached. My mind raced. I kept thinking about my own daughter—about how I felt when she skinned her knees or someone was mean to her at class. I felt afraid to even imagine how I would feel if anything similar happened to her.

"I can't say how sorry I am," I finally said. "I would love to pray for her."

"OK," she said, not bothering to wipe the tears anymore. "I'll get her."

I felt terrified the moment she left the room. My heart raced. My mind ached. What could I possibly say that could help? How could I come across as anything but condescending when speaking into a depth of trauma so much deeper than I had ever experienced?

~

People are sometimes scared when they meet me, usually because they are worried I am going to see some horrible demon or spiritual wound on them. Though I see both these things frequently, they almost never lead me to judgment. The truth is, when you really and honestly see the pain and the fruits of pain in others, it creates the purest compassion and the deepest empathy.

Knowing this, some cowardly and pathetic part of me did not want to see what this girl was going through. I was afraid to see her wounds, afraid to feel compassion and empathy for such agony. I knew that it was not my job to fix her. I knew that I couldn't. I knew that all I had to do was hear what God had to say, and I knew that He would speak, but still I was afraid.

Suddenly the doors burst open, and, startled, I completely shut off my ability to see in the spirit as the woman walked in. Her daughter was behind her, and a family friend joined them, following with a tender hand on the young girl's back.

The anxiety rushing through my veins vanished in an instant, replaced by a slow, deep ache. Everything about the young girl's expression, posture, and stance screamed of deepest anguish. Her eyes shifted back and forth constantly, moving between the ground, the ceiling, and somewhere in the distance, never meeting mine. She crossed her arms across her chest, and then she fidgeted with her hands in front of her, shifting her feet with every breath.

A primal empathy welled up in my soul. It was deeper than the empathy of a minister, even deeper than the empathy of a father with a daughter of his own. It came from my very foundation—one human capable of feeling pain recognizing another human feeling deep pain. Every part of me wanted to help, but every part didn't know how.

"Here she is," her mother said, making every effort to sound jovial.

"All right," I said. "Let's pray."

I asked for God to release His truth into the room and equip us all to hear His voice clearly.

It was painful to look at the young woman, even without looking in the spirit. Fear screamed through my whole body—that intense sense of not wanting to subject myself to more of the pain I was already feeling. But courage—from where I still don't know—lit up the very center of my heart, reminding me if I had even a single grain of encouragement or hope for this girl, it was worth whatever pain I would experience in giving it to her.

Wanting to take it in stride, I looked down at the ground and looked in the spirit, deciding it would be easier if I started with her feet and worked my way up, rather than activating my gift while looking straight at her. Her wounds were so severe that the blood running down her legs was filling both of her gray tennis shoes. The pain I felt while looking at her in the physical doubled, then tripled. It was so intense that it threw me off balance. Every other sensation shut down in the face of such impossible pain.

I clenched my eyes, unable to handle the sorrow. It overwhelmed everything, but it did not snuff out the candle of courage at the center of my heart. Before I could doubt or think, I snapped both eyes wide open and looked directly at her face.

Even as I write this now, my breath leaves me at the memory of what I saw.

She was perfect.

She was absolutely perfect in every way—without a single flaw. She looked as perfect as my own daughter did the day she was born. There was not a single scratch or scrape on her. There was nothing wrong with her at all.

I was stunned. I was baffled, confused. In the physical I could see the way she was looking around, the way she was cringing away from me. She was hurt. She was in pain. But she was perfect. She was unharmed. Nothing was wrong.

Some part of me could still feel the pain. It was distant. I had to focus on it to feel it was there. It was as if it were being drowned out by her sheer perfection. It was then I realized what was happening. I was seeing her how God saw her.

It was beyond understanding—both bigger and smaller than I can put into words. He was not covering up the pain. He was not hiding it or hiding from it. It actually felt as if He were right in the middle of it, as if He were feeling it more than I was and even more than she was. He was not covering it up. He was just better than it—not superior to it, not above it, not too tough for it, just better. He could somehow stand at the very center of all that pain and remain good.

It wasn't fake. It wasn't makeup over a bruise. He really saw her as the most perfect and beautiful thing that had ever existed, and He saw every moment of everything that happened at the same time. Somehow His goodness was better than all that darkness.

My mind was not built to understand what I was seeing. I could not justify the discrepancy between what I saw in the physical, what my empathy was screaming, and the truth of how God saw the situation. I did not know how to bottle it up into words and give it to her. I did not know if she would or even could receive it in the midst of so much pain. But I did my best to say what I saw.

Wounds are an inevitable part of life on earth. Some of us experience more wounds than others; some of us experience more severe wounds than others. But regardless of how frequent or deep our wounds are, God's capacity for restoration is infinite.

I love inner healing ministries, I love support groups, I love counseling, I love self-help books, I love personality assessments, and I love therapy. These are all wonderful tools for learning to build healthy lives. But nothing outmatches the healing power of our Father's perfect love. And any ministry, group, counselor, book, assessment, or therapist that does not make connecting you with that incredible love its highest priority will never give you true wholeness. These things may give you insight into how you work and may help you cope with your pains and fears, but they will not give you health. They cannot—not the kind of health I saw in that girl.

You might be thinking, "What health? She was still in pain. She still experienced trauma."

To this day I cannot reconcile the fact of her pain and the truth of what God saw in her. I do know, however, beyond all doubt that what I saw was true. When I remember her pain and the pain I felt in empathy, it feels like a memory similar to recalling moments of pain or fear from my childhood. I can remember feeling it, but I do not feel it now. When I remember the goodness I saw in her, it is as if she is standing right in front of me. It does not feel like a memory at all. It feels as tangible as the air moving through my lungs or the pressure of my feet touching the floor.

God is good. God is in control. God is love. God has a plan. God is the answer. Most Christians would agree with all those statements, but it is easy to see how in the face of tragedy each could feel like a little bandage with pictures of cartoon characters stuck to a broken leg—cute but basically useless. I know how positivity and Christian clichés can feel like lemon juice on a paper cut when you are in the middle of a crisis or pain, but I would hate for over-familiarity with sentiments about God's nature to sabotage an experience with the reality of His nature.

Call it positivity, insensitivity, minimization, or whatever else, but when I experienced how God saw that young woman in the midst of her pain, every cheesy sentiment I ever heard about His goodness rang pure and true, much as every cheesy thing my parents used to say about how much they loved me suddenly rang true when I first held my own child in my arms.

God is better than we could ever imagine Him to be. It is just true. He has an answer for every pain, failure, disappointment, tragedy, disaster, trauma, injustice, and fear. Not a fake answer, not a blanket statement, not a cheesy one-liner—He has something real. We just have to let Him show us. He paid dearly for the right to be present in the midst of our greatest tragedy and pain. He paid for the right to release His light into the very center of our deepest darkness. He paid with His Son's blood, the highest price that could be paid. Wounds are an inevitable part of life on earth, but He paid for the right to heal every one of them.

I know the burden of pain and trauma. I have seen it. But I know that God's goodness outweighs the sum of all suffering. I have seen it. His goodness is mysterious, and it accomplishes the impossible. I can write about it, pastors can teach about it, mentors can coach us toward it, but only God can introduce us to His profound good.

Thoughts to Ponder

- Take a moment and think about what it means for God to remain good without distancing Himself from pain.

- Remember some of the wounds or pain that you have experienced in your own life. Pause and ask God how His goodness is present in those areas right now.

- God's goodness is vast and mysterious. It is much larger than our understanding of the word *good*. Mysteries as immense as the nature of God's goodness are not meant to be resolved in a few minutes—they are meant to be revealed, layer by layer, over a lifetime. Bring your mind back to the subject of His goodness as you read the next chapters and over the next few days. See if meditating on His goodness presents more opportunities to uncover more of the mystery of His goodness.

GOLDEN CAGES

A FEW YEARS AGO OUR church hosted a gathering of church leaders from all around the southeastern region of the United States. I volunteered to help by running some of the audiovisual elements needed for the meeting, so I arrived early to set up all the equipment.

Angels moved around as the band members set up their instruments and the rest of the production team ran cables and set up speakers. Some were worship angels, running through the steps and dances they were planning to do during the worship portion of the meeting. They ran from one side of the room to the other with long, ribbony pieces of fabric dragging through the air behind them as they twisted, turned, and jumped through the air. Others were angels of intercession. They pressed their hands on each chair one at a time, leaving bright, glowing handprints wherever they touched. Still others were preparing the room in other ways, lining the side walls with broad golden bowls and filling them with some kind of light-green liquid. Another group of angels was laying out trays with small tools on them. The tools made me think of dental or surgical tools, minus the inherent terror those implements evoke.

Some of what was happening was familiar to me. Although something new and different happens at every worship service I attend, many of the overall themes are similar or at least on the same grid. The bowls and tools were a little outside the norm, but I had learned not to dwell too long on trying to figure out every detail of why things look a certain way; those meanings tend to emerge naturally as things continue.

I am always humbled when I see how thoroughly and consistently the host of heaven prepare for God's children to gather. It doesn't matter how big or small the gathering is—whether it is a church service, small group, or something else—the angels always put their all into preparing for what God is ready to do.

Soon the leaders began to arrive. They were mostly pastors from many different churches from all over the region. Some were surprisingly young; some were surprisingly old. Some brought their spouses; some came alone. Some came dressed in suits and ties; some came in Hawaiian shirts and flip-flops. The one consistent feature that caught my eye as the room began to fill was that each and every leader who came into the room was bruised, battered, and beaten up when I looked at him or her in the spirit.

Some only had some light bruising around their cheeks and eyes; others looked like they fell into a rock tumbler on their way in. Many of them had small cuts and nicks, but some had deep gouges. Some had arrows in their backs; others had daggers. Even some of their clothes looked ruffled and torn in places. Their appearance did not shock me. I have seen plenty of people with varying degrees of hurts and wounds in the spirit. What surprised me was how consistently wounded every person who came into the room was.

I have been a pastor's kid and/or a missionary kid for

the majority of my life. I am very aware of the kind of bumps and bruises one can receive when leading a church. But I was very surprised to see the extent of those hurts gathered up in one place.

The service began with one of our church network leaders welcoming everyone. He reminded them the main goal of the event was to create an opportunity for all of them to connect and for us to bless and serve them as fellow leaders in the church.

Worship began. All the angels in the room began dancing and moving in time with the music, following the choreography they practiced earlier but still improvising and adding little flairs here and there.

Some say worship is about us showing our adoration for God. This is true, but it is a bit incomplete based on my experience. Every time I see people worship, it is like a giant corporate dance. The people extend their affections, some by dancing and singing, some in ways subtler and more internal. This pulls on heaven, and heaven responds. The presence of God enters the room in response to the worship, and the angels' dancing intensifies. This causes the worship coming from the people to grow, which in turn pulls on heaven even more. Every time is different, of course. Sometimes God's presence initiates this push and pull of affection. Sometimes the angels seem to be kickstarting the momentum with what they are doing. And sometimes the energy of the congregation, the presence of God, and the dance of angels all initiate together at the same time. This service was an example of the latter.

~

I could feel the hunger for more of God's presence emanating from each person in the room. It was like a rhythmic
inhale and exhale that set every spiritual thing in the room
glowing like coals from a fire. Immediately the angels began
dancing with an intensity that matched the feeling of hunger
swelling from every direction. A bright light appeared at the
front of the room—so bright I couldn't look at it without
squinting. Billows of white and gold cloud poured out from
the light, filling the room with a staggering sense of peace.

All around the room I watched everyone relax. Tight
shoulders loosened. People rolled their necks and stretched
their arms. As they did, their wounds began to open up
and bleed. Immediately more angels entered the room in
sets of two. One of each pair picked up one of the trays of
the tools laid out earlier, and the other grabbed a bowl of
the green liquid.

These duos made their way around the room from
person to person, stopping at each to tend the bleeding
wounds. They cleaned the wounds with green liquid from
the bowls and used the tools to remove arrows from backs
and old bandages from open gashes. Bruises were wiped
away as easily as dry-erase marker under the influence of
the green liquid. The angels stitched anything that needed
stitching, bandaged anything that needed bandaging, and
cleaned anything that needed cleaning.

It was interesting to me that the wounds started bleeding
when everyone in the room was most at rest. It was as if
they had all been doing their best to hold it together and

were only able to truly let go in an environment such as the one that day. It can be hard to recognize the kinds of pressures and expectations put on leaders. We expect them to have it together. We expect them to have a good plan. We expect them to be generous. We expect them to be kind. We expect them to be thoughtful. We expect them to be patient. We expect them to be decisive, personable, strong, gentle, honest, straightforward, good public speakers, insightful counselors, dynamic visionaries, and excellent managers, all while having great relationships with their spouses and kids. And when they do not meet those expectations, regardless of whether we communicated them or not, we are hurt and disappointed. I believe leaders in the body of Christ are called to a high level of living, but sometimes I wonder how responsible we are as followers for empowering them to reach that standard of life and character.

Within a few minutes every wound was either covered in clean bandages or completely gone. The cloud pouring into the room began to flow in more thickly, covering the floor in a gold and white glow. The whole room felt even more at rest, as if a big weight had finally been set down. As this new level of comfort and peace settled in, I saw Jesus step into the room.

He walked up to a man in the second row. He put His hands on both sides of the man's face, looked into his eyes, and then kissed the man on the top of his head. Then He touched the center of the man's chest with the tips of the fingers of His right hand. He straightened each finger out and moved His hand down the middle of the man's torso in a slow chopping motion. The man's chest swung open like a gate.

I could see into the man's chest cavity, but there was nothing gross about it. For whatever reason it looked like something his chest was designed to do. I noticed that his heart was in a cage. It was small and metal, a little like a birdcage. It was dented, bent, and twisted as if a wild animal had been desperately trying to get into it.

With absolute precision and gentleness Jesus reached forward, opened the broken cage, and removed it from the man's chest without the sides touching his heart at all. He handed the cage to an angel standing just behind Him and then leaned forward and took the man's heart in His hands. He lifted the heart to His mouth and blew on it. Like a coal catching oxygen from the wind, the man's heart heated and began to glow.

Then Jesus did something that surprised me. He reached behind His back and pulled out a golden cage. It was similar in size and shape to the one He had removed, except that it was in perfect condition and much more ornate than the first one had likely ever been. He placed the man's heart in the golden cage and returned it to his chest.

Jesus went from person to person, going through more or less the exact same process with each one. Some He greeted with warm hugs, others with a kiss on the cheek, and still others by cupping their chins in His hand like an adoring grandparent with a beloved grandchild. With each one, however, He removed a dented cage from the person's chest, blew on his or her heart, and placed the heart in a new golden cage.

I watched Him carefully as He went, still feeling baffled. I had assumed the cage was a bad thing—the man's attempt at protecting his heart from the pressures of leading and the harsh responses people sometimes have toward leaders. Even if that were true—the cage representing an earthly form of protection—it still surprised me that Jesus would provide a replacement cage.

I looked at the expression of compassion that came across Jesus' face as He looked into the eyes of one of the pastors. I saw the glint of empathy in His eyes as He slipped the heart into a golden cage and carefully hung it back in the man's chest. He knew. He understood the place they were in. He knew where He was sending them and whom He was sending them to. He knew that where they were going, these pastors would need to guard their hearts.

Part of me wishes we could all operate in perfect empathy: the ones following able to understand and share the feelings of the ones leading, the ones leading able to understand and share the feelings of the ones following, all expectations communicated up front, and every violation of those expectations communicated with kindness and vulnerability. But that is not the world we live in right now.

I found it comforting that Jesus provided a way to protect their hearts from the kind of opposition those smashed and twisted cages represented, though I long for a day when that kind of covering is no longer necessary.

Thoughts to Ponder

- If we want to experience the fullness of God's goodness, then we are going to have to be willing to let that goodness change the way we act and think.

- Knowing how God responds to our hurts and pains is just as important as knowing how He responds to the hurts and pains in others.

- Pick someone you know—a friend, coworker, leader, or neighbor—and start asking the Lord how He is manifesting His goodness in the person's life.

THE QUIZ

I STARTED MY FIRST YEAR at the Bethel School of Supernatural Ministry (BSSM) in Redding, California, when I was nineteen. I noticed within a few months that they had a big challenge on their hands. The goal of the school was to train up revivalists, people trained "to continue in the ministry style of Jesus: to enjoy the presence of God, say what He is saying, and do what He is doing."[1] This mission attracted a wide variety of people. Some had been pastors and leaders in the church for decades, and some had only known Jesus for a few months. With such a wide variety of backgrounds, experiences, and perspectives in play, it can be difficult to create a curriculum that speaks to every kind of student.

To this end, one of the teachers at the school, Dann Farrelly, came up with a simple quiz to help ensure that every student had at least a basic understanding of biblical history. BSSM is not a traditional Bible school—it mainly focuses on hands-on training with the prophetic, healing, and learning to live from one's God-given identity, but Dann wanted to make sure that, even though the information would be redundant for many students, everyone had a good baseline to work from.

The quiz was given about two months into our first year of school. It consisted of a basic timeline of biblical history from Abraham to the present day, as well as a map of Israel and the Middle East in the times of the Bible.

The day of the quiz started quite normally. It was Tuesday, and on Tuesdays we always started with worship led by a team of my fellow students. On this particular day worship completely took off instantly. The tangible presence of God came immediately and fervently, causing almost all of the 250 students in the room to begin dancing.

Though I have a very full and rich worship relationship with God, I very rarely do much of anything that reveals externally what is happening internally. On this day, however, the sense of joy and celebration that entered the room caused even me to start jumping and dancing around.

A thick flow of golden oil came pouring in from behind the stage, filling the entire room up to my knees. All of the running and dancing caused the oil to slosh back and forth in rolling waves that sent splashes in every direction. More than a dozen angels were joining in on the celebration. They ran from one side of the room to the other, playfully kicking and splashing the oil into people's faces as they went.

More angels came in carrying massive barrels filled with even more oil. Some poured the oil directly on some of the dancing students, and I even saw one angel smash an entire barrel of oil over a student's head.

A crack began to form on the wall behind the stage. Impossibly bright beams of light shot through the opening seam, bringing with them an even stronger sense of anticipation for what this level of worship could release into the room. The dancing and singing only grew increasingly fervent as we moved from song to song. The band members were dancing so wildly that they were getting tangled in their guitar cords. The feeling of acceleration in worship was intoxicating, rising higher and higher with no sign of stopping.

~

A figure emerged out of the beautiful chaos of dancing students, flowing oil, and celebrating angels. Dann Farrelly stepped onto the stage, a thick three-ring binder tucked under his arm.

I had completely forgotten about the quiz. My eyes darted up to the clock. It was the time worship was scheduled to end. The power of worship beating like a drum in my chest, I looked back at Dann, confident he was going to let worship continue. There had already been moments in class when the schedule changed because the presence of the Holy Spirit showed up. As Dann approached the microphone, I stood with the certainty that we would have the opportunity to see where the momentum of our worship would take us.

Instead, Dann leaned into the microphone and said, "All right, everyone, go ahead and find your seat. We are going to go ahead and get started with our quiz."

Half the room let out an audible gasp, including me. The band members looked at one another as if to say, "Should we just keep going?" not because of any disrespect toward Dann but because the momentum of our worship had been so palpable. Stopping almost felt like a crime.

Dann seemed to detect our collective uncertainty, "Yes," he said in a gentle tone, "please find your seats."

After a few seconds' hesitation, everyone began shuffling back to his or her seat. A handful of interns passed out the quiz, a single sheet of paper printed on both sides, and we all got out our pencils and began filling in the blanks. Minutes passed. I finished filling out the timeline, but I still couldn't get over what had happened. Worship really felt as if it was going somewhere. When I stopped and thought about it, it felt as if worship could still go somewhere. I looked around the room and saw that all the angels present during worship were still in the room. They were right where they had been when Dann told us to return to our seats, looking as if they were waiting for something to happen. I even saw one angel balancing on one foot with a large barrel over his head, frozen in mid-pour.

Looking at the angels caused the feeling I felt during worship to begin to grow. I looked at the crack in the back wall. Beams of light still shone through the opening, carrying a sense of impossible joy and excitement.

Seeing all the angels waiting and feeling the regret that came from not knowing what was on the other side of that crack in the wall, I made up my mind. Dann made a mistake. We should have kept worshipping. This was just some simple quiz. We could have easily rescheduled it. What we had been doing was way more important.

My self-righteous internal monologue was suddenly interrupted by a gentle tug at the edge of my consciousness. With the lightest possible of touches, I felt the Holy Spirit draw my gaze to the back corner of the room. There

I saw a three-tiered fountain overflowing with a thick green liquid. Three angels stood at the edge of the fountain, catching the overflow in large wooden buckets. As soon as a bucket was full, one of the angels would carry it to the far wall and set it down next to a long line of already full buckets.

As I watched this three-angel bucket brigade do its work, snapshots of X-rays, old sports injuries, bacteria, viruses, and genetic abnormalities began filling my mind. My eyes snapped to my fellow students. Suddenly I could see straight through them. I could see the buildup of plaque in arteries near the heart, tendons that were pulling incorrectly, and misaligned vertebrae putting pressure on the spine. My eyes shot from ailment to ailment like a bloodhound with its nose set to "illness."

I could feel God's desire to heal these people, even the ones who were not sick. When I looked at them, I began to see pictures of sick relatives, friends, or acquaintances. The overwhelming drive of God's desire to heal was strong enough to make me consider slipping out of my seat to go lay my hands on a few of the people who caught my eye.

Just as this feeling reached its peak, another gentle tug pulled my attention to the opposite corner of the room, to the right of the stage. There I saw a small hole in the ceiling. Through the opening I saw layers and layers of swirling clouds and sunshine. As I looked, letters began pouring through the opening, the white envelopes signed by hand and sealed with bright-red wax. The letters fluttered into the room and then sailed off in different directions, each coming to a stop over a different person's head.

Watching this caused prophetic words to fill my mind. Promises of future victories, deeply personal affirmations of value, and poetic declarations of fatherly love all fought to be first to settle into my attention. More and more letters came flooding into the room. Soon dozens were clustered above each person, with even more on the way. I couldn't focus on anyone for more than a second without having three or four visions, impressions, or sentences in a still, small voice crowd into my psyche. It was then I began to catch on to what the Holy Spirit was saying.

~

I looked at all the angels that were present during worship. I felt the sense of acceleration I felt while we were worshipping. I looked at the fountain where the angels were filling up buckets. I felt God's relentless desire to heal. I looked at the hole in the ceiling where the letters were pouring in. I felt God's desire to speak to His children. Then I looked at Dann.

He had set his big binder on a circular table on the stage and was going over his notes. As I watched him flip through the pages, I noticed an angel that had missed my attention earlier standing just behind him. The angel would not have looked out of place in a Victorian library. His multilayered clothing was all tucked, tied, and placed with precision and care. He wore a pair of thin golden glasses attached to his coat by a fine silver chain, and a thick forest-green book rested under his arm. He walked forward and laid the book on the table next to Dann's notes. I just had time to see the word *Life* stenciled in thick gold letters on the book's spine before the angel flopped it open, kicking a puff of fine dust into the air.

After a few moments words from the book began to peel off the page line by line and float into the air. They were not written in any language I had ever seen before, though with the way they shifted and twisted through the air as they moved, I doubt I could have read them even if they were in a language I knew. More and more words emerged from the book, creating a floating swarm around Dann and the angel. Once every word left the open page, the angel turned to the next. As soon as he did, the words in the air swam out into the crowd. They darted in all directions without hesitation, sinking straight through the skin of anyone they touched. Some of the words sank into people's heads, others into their stomachs, and still others went and wrapped themselves around people's feet. One line of unfamiliar text soared toward me and went directly into the center of my chest.

A strange sensation ran all through me. Stories I had heard during church as a child came rushing into my mind. Scriptures I had not thought about in years began reciting themselves in my memory. Each story and each scripture came to me in a crisp, clear light. They had dimension and impact that had been lost with the familiarity I developed with them over the years. I could see how one Bible story connected to the next and how it connected to all the others. I was receiving a completely new level of appreciation and understanding of God's written Word. And then it hit me.

God is big.

In fact, maybe He is so big that He is 100 percent ready to release a new level of breakthrough in worship, 100 percent ready to release supernatural physical healing, 100 percent ready to release prophetic declarations, and also 100 percent ready to release a new level of wisdom regarding the Bible, all at the same time.

I was arrogant to think my ability to see what God was doing was more valid than Dann's ability to see what He was doing. We are finite beings serving an infinite God. It only makes sense that our perception of Him and the things He does would be subject to the same limitations that apply to other parts of our lives. However, when we learn to honor the ways other people see God, we have the opportunity to receive the benefit of what they see.

As I handed in my finished quiz, I realized one more thing. I would have known how to pursue a new level of worship. Because of my time at the school of ministry, I would have known how to pursue supernatural healing. I would have known how to pursue a new level of awareness of God's voice. But I would not have known how to pursue the next level of biblical wisdom, at least not without Dann's help. By honoring him, even begrudgingly, I was given access to something I would not have been able to receive on my own.

That is the point of gathering together and pursuing God. Sure, you can have a full and rich relationship just between you and God. You can get all the best sermons and teachings through a podcast or live stream, but that is not the only point. I had already learned every piece of information Dann put on the quiz back when I was a kid in Sunday school. The revelation I was receiving was not about the quality or newness of the information—it was about my recognition and honor of the gift on Dann's life.

Even if you read all the best books, listened to all the best messages, and studied the Bible without ceasing, there would still be aspects of God's nature you would miss out on, because some of the best pictures of His nature can only be found in the hearts of His children.

The librarian angel closed the thick green book as I finished pondering this. He hesitated for a moment, giving me plenty of time to reread the word embossed on the book's spine, *Life*, and then he tucked it under his arm, lowered his glasses, and looked me straight in the eye with a satisfied smile on his face. I guess I managed to pass two quizzes.

Thoughts to Ponder

- If God can be doing more than one thing at once, then how do we know what the "right" thing to do is?

- I shared an example of the kind of benefit that can come from honoring a Bible teacher. What other kinds of benefits do you imagine could come from honoring other kinds of gifts?

- Do you think the Holy Spirit corrected my attitude because Dann was right and I was wrong, or did He have a different reason for correcting me?

THE STONE HOOD

WHEN I WAS NINETEEN, I went on a mission trip to Mexico. On one of the nights, we hosted an outdoor event in the middle of downtown Tijuana. We got approval from city officials to use a stage in one of the town squares to play worship music, preach the gospel, and pray for sick people to be healed. I was not on the worship team or one of the people preaching, so I stood out in the square with a dozen or so others, waiting for people to show up so we could ask them if they wanted prayer. I tend to be socially anxious and introverted at the best of times, so having to constantly ask people I didn't know, in a language I didn't know well, if they wanted prayer was a real stretch for me. But I kept at it with as much courage and care as I could muster. Passersby began to stop and receive prayer a few at a time, but after an hour or so we ran into a problem.

Thick, dark clouds filled every corner of the sky, and soon thick drops of rain began to fall. The heavy flow of street traffic that had been causing the pavilion to fill with people began to get lighter and lighter as pedestrians ran for cover under awnings or marched onward, in too big a hurry to avoid the rain to see or hear what we were doing.

Just as the crowd began to dissipate, one of the people onstage grabbed a microphone. "Everyone," he said, "we are not going to let this rain stop what God is wanting to do here tonight." He then jabbed a finger up at the sky and yelled, "Do you want to see a miracle? Rain, we command you to stop in the name of Jesus!"

"Oh no," I thought. "This is going to be super embarrassing." Despite my almost complete lack of faith that anything would happen, I couldn't help but draw my gaze upward as the young man began to pray.

I saw four angels ascending from near the stage. Each had broad golden wings, was wearing a gold robe, and had a gold band in its hair. As they drifted to the four corners of the city square, each was also holding a thin golden staff with ornate swirling patterns embossed on it from end to end.

They flew up about fifty feet in the air and hovered at the corners of the square, each holding its staff vertically so one end pointed to the sky and one pointed to the ground. There was a bright flash as each staff ignited with light and shot a beam of light that connected the four angels in a perfect square. The light was gone as fast as the flash from a camera, and the angels descended and landed back on the stage.

After thirty seconds I stopped feeling drops of rain on my shoulders and face. In another thirty seconds the clouds began to thin. A few minutes after that there was a perfectly square hole in the clouds over the area where we were ministering. The sky was filled with dark clouds as far as I could see except for the area above us, where I could see hundreds of stars shining through.

Then, instead of running past it to get out of the rain, dozens and dozens of people flocked to the area around the stage because it was now the only place they could go to stay dry. Inspired and energized by seeing such a dramatic miracle, I dove back into praying for people with fervor. I prayed for people with asthma. I prayed for people on crutches. I prayed for people with cancer. Then I saw a man come stumbling out of a bar into the square, drunk and confused. A feeling of compassion welled up in my soul as I watched him try to make his way through the crowd. I rushed over to him and, without really thinking about what I was doing, gave him a full-armed hug. I started telling him how much God loved him. When the limits of my Spanish inhibited me from saying more, I switched to English and continued telling him about God's love. I watched as the drunk man's eyes cleared, his posture straightened, and his balance was restored. He looked at me as I spoke, making no sign as to whether he understood me or not, but when I finished, he immediately approached the stage and began worshipping with the group up front.

Even more energized by this, I searched the crowd for the next person. Immediately I saw another drunk man enter the square from the opposite side. I pushed my way through the growing crowd, feeling an even deeper compassion swelling in my heart as I approached. I tapped the man on the shoulder, and he turned and looked at me. As my eyes met his, I felt the well of compassion in my heart explode in a thousand directions at once. I could feel God's insatiable desire to pour out His love on this man. I could feel the incredible anticipation God had for this moment when He and this man would finally have the opportunity to be reconciled.

Vision after vision of this man's future flew in front of my eyes. I saw him leading people to Jesus by the dozens, then the hundreds, and then the thousands. I saw him

leading an entire generation of young men into righteous-
ness and purity. I saw him being a key part in a revival
that would sweep across the entire country of Mexico.
Each vision was so vivid and real that not only could I
see how it would happen; I could feel the grace God had
appointed to empower it to happen. I could feel the very
essence of the plan of God aligning with this man's life,
empowering him to step into the fullness of his destiny.

My Spanish was far too weak to express even the barest
corner of what I was seeing and feeling, so I trusted that
what I was about to say was more about imparting grace
than understanding content, and I began prophesying to
him in English. Almost instantly his eyes began to clear
and focus. The reddish flush on his face and the smell of
alcohol on his breath began to fade. His eyes locked with
mine as I continued pouring every ounce of what I was
feeling and seeing into rapid-fire prophetic declarations.

I felt perfectly in line with the heated rhythm of compassion, love, and hope beating in my heart as I spoke.
It felt as though a river were flowing into me and then
through me at ten thousand gallons a second. I watched as
dawning understanding spread across the man's expression and tears began to form at the corners of his eyes. I
continued on until the last drop of that river of life had
passed through me, and then I took in a deep breath,
resting my hand on the man's shoulder.

We stood there silently staring at one another for a
few moments, but then a casing of dark stone rolled from
behind his back and locked into place in front of his face,
like some strange combination of the hood of a sweatshirt

and a motorcycle helmet, hard and dark as onyx. I shut off my ability to see in the spirit so I could see his face. Tears still resting in the corners of his eyes, he shook his head, said, "No, gracias," and turned and walked back the way he came.

~

I stood frozen as I watched him disappear into the crowd. Numbness slowly gave way to a deep, overwhelming ache, causing me to stumble my way to a corner to the right of the stage, where a few of my fellow teammates were sitting down to rest. I crumpled down into a ball near their feet and sobbed for the rest of the night.

People sometimes ask me if it is hard to see in the spirit. They usually ask this because they are concerned that seeing demons would be too frightening or seeing spiritual wounds on people would be too overwhelming. The truth is that I am rarely bothered by seeing demons or wounds. This is partially because after seeing the enemy's tactics so many times over so many years, I am no longer impressed or surprised by what demons do, but mostly because God has a perfect plan, ready and waiting to be released, for every wound and every demonic attack. The most painful thing I see is how abundantly God releases His goodness on His people and how frequently that profound good goes unnoticed or unclaimed.

I have been in meetings where people pray for financial breakthrough. It comes every time, but I do not see a change in every person's finances every time. Sometimes the reasons are obvious. Sometimes financial breakthrough looks like a sudden windfall or an unexpected check in the mail in a moment of need. Sometimes financial breakthrough looks like business plans and ideas. Sometimes financial provision looks like the grace to change spending habits and manage debt. It can be easy to miss God's goodness when it does not show up the way we expect or if we do not realize the manifestation of His goodness often involves action on our part.

I certainly was not positioning myself to see God's goodness when my teammate got up to pray against the rain. I was more ready to feel embarrassed than to experience a miracle. In fact, I suspect those angels with the golden staffs were standing behind my friend when he got up to pray. I did not see them because I did not believe or expect them to be there. It wasn't until I did an action of faith—the admittedly small action of looking up as he prayed—that I saw the angels being released to fulfill his prayers.

That is not to say we should be worried that we are constantly undermining the plans of God with our inaction or wrong action. That kind of thinking tends to land us with false responsibility and paralyze us with fear. Instead, we need to recognize we are on a persistent journey of discovering how good God is and how to partner with Him to release that goodness on earth. I think that is why the apostle Paul says this:

> Do not be conformed to this world, but be transformed by the renewing of your mind, that you may prove what is the good and acceptable and perfect will of God.
> —ROMANS 12:2, MEV

We have to let the goodness of God renew our minds, to change what we expect to happen with us and to the world. If we don't, then we may not recognize His goodness when it comes. We may even reject it.

Thoughts to Ponder

- You may have noticed that after experiencing the miracle with the rain, I began to be much bolder with the ways I was praying for others, acting well outside the boundaries of my usual personality. Why do you think experiencing miracles increases boldness, and how do you think you would react if you were in the same situation?

- How could you position yourself so that you could have the opportunity to see a miracle happen?

- Despite the feeling of connection that I had with the drunk man, he decided not to receive what God was ready to release on him. Why do you think this happened?

- Are there areas where you find it difficult to receive from God?

- How could you position yourself to run headlong into those areas where it is hard for you to receive from Him?

ACTIVATION AND STUDY— REVELATION

ONE OF MY FAVORITE BIBLE stories about seeing in the spirit comes from 2 Kings 6. The king of Aram was at war with Israel, and it was proving difficult. Every time he set a trap or ambush, the Israelite army would be on extra guard or simply avoid the area entirely. Frustrated by the repeated sabotage of his plans, the king of Aram called a council of his officers, asking which of them was a traitor spying for the king of Israel.

One of the officers said there was no spy among them, "but Elisha, the prophet who is in Israel, tells the king of Israel the very words you speak in your bedroom" (2 Kings 6:12).

Understandably perturbed by the idea of someone undermining all his best-laid plans, the king of Aram ordered his men to capture Elisha. Soon his men were able to discover where Elisha was living. They sent chariots, horsemen, and a strong force to surround the city in the dead of night.

The next morning Elisha's servant woke up and went outside, only to find that the entire city had been surrounded by a great army. Alarmed, the servant rushed back inside to wake his master.

> "Don't be afraid," the prophet answered. "Those who are with us are more than those who are with them."

> And Elisha prayed, "Open his eyes, LORD, so that
> he may see." Then the LORD opened the servant's
> eyes, and he looked and saw the hills full of horses
> and chariots of fire all around Elisha.
>
> —2 KINGS 6:16–17

The enemy soldiers charged forward, seeing their target within their grasp, but the prophet prayed, and every one of the soldiers was struck with blindness. He then led them all to Samaria, where the king of Israel and his army were waiting.

Elisha prayed again, after he had led them into the midst of the king's men, and the Aramean soldiers' eyes were opened again. The king of Israel, seeing that his enemy was at his mercy, asked Elisha, "Shall I kill them?" (2 Kings 6:21).

"Do not kill them," the prophet answered. "Would you kill those you have captured with your own sword or bow? Set food and water before them so that they may eat and drink and then go back to their master" (2 Kings 6:22).

So the king had a great feast prepared for the captured soldiers, and once they had eaten their fill, he sent them back to their own king. After that, Aram stopped sending marauding parties into the land of Israel.

This is a wonderful example not only of the gift of seeing in the spirit but of how revelation transforms our perspective. Elisha's servant sees the enemy soldiers surrounding the city and is understandably frightened. But Elisha says there are more with them than against them and then prays that the servant's eyes will be opened. The servant then sees their attackers are surrounded by an even greater spiritual force.

Now let's stop here for one second. This is a popular and famous story from the Bible, so there is a good chance you were already familiar with how the story ends before we got there. But pause for a moment and put yourself in the shoes of Elisha's servant. You just discovered you are surrounded by enemies. Then God reveals a great vision—you are surrounded by an army of supernatural protectors. What do you expect to happen next?

If you are anything like me, you expect the army of fiery angels to fall upon your foes as they make their charge. You expect a dramatic display of God's might as your enemies are slain before you, an incredible last-minute moment of divine intervention. But as you know, that is not what happens.

The chariots of fire and horses don't seem to factor into what happens next at all. Elisha prays, the soldiers are immediately struck blind, and the prophet of the Lord hoodwinks the entire enemy army, leading them into the camp of the king of Israel. There they are offered food and drink and then sent home.

Elisha saw a great deal of God's power displayed on the earth. He followed the prophet Elijah and learned much. He experienced several miracles that were released through his own hands and declared many powerful prophecies. Elisha let revelation transform him.

There is no specific record of whether God told Elisha directly how to respond to the attackers, or if Elisha had simply seen the work of the Lord's hand often enough to recognize where the encounter was intended to go.

My version of being delivered from this crisis would have ended with many dead Arameans and a very upset king of Aram. Elisha's version ended this way: "So the bands from Aram stopped raiding Israel's territory" (2 Kings 6:23). Some scholars believe it was well over a year before the king of Aram made any further attempts to attack Israel.

My best-case scenario would have involved the death of the enemy army. God's best-case scenario involved no shedding of blood and a feast. My best-case scenario would have weakened the enemy army and hindered its ability to attack. God's best-case scenario ended the enemy's desire to attack and ended hostilities for quite some time.

God's Nature

Elisha's many encounters with the Lord taught him to look not just for God's hand but His nature. The chariots of fire were not present for the Arameans' destruction but for Elisha's protection. From a human perspective we might assume those things would be the same, but God saw it differently, and, because he was looking and listening, so did Elisha.

There are two definitions of the English word *revelation* that I like:

1. The making known of something that was previously secret or unknown

2. The divine or supernatural disclosure to humans of something relating to human existence or the world[2]

Revelation is God revealing to us how He relates to us. It is God showing us how He works, how the world works, and where He placed us in relation to both. This information is often secret—not because He wishes to hide but because He understands the power of discovery. We must remember, we are finite people in relationship with an infinite God. I cannot currently imagine a model of the universe where a real relationship with a God as awesome as ours could happen any other way than through a steady process of revelation, a slow unveiling.

I like to compare the process of revelation to an Easter egg hunt. If the goal of an Easter egg hunt is to hide eggs from my children, then I can succeed in that goal every time. Why? Because I will get a shovel and bury some ten feet under the ground, I will get a ladder and hide some on the top of my roof, and I will get a box and mail the rest to Mongolia. Thankfully for my children's sake, the point of an Easter egg hunt is not that the eggs are hidden but that they are found.

However, being a father who likes to bring joy to his children, I do not just pile the eggs in the middle of the lawn and call it a day. I place the eggs where it is within their ability to find them but also where they will have to use the full capacity of their developing minds to discover them. Where I hide the Easter eggs has changed as my children have grown. Most of them used to be spread across the lawn, with a few hidden partway under rocks or in bushes. Later I started hiding them in the low branches of trees, under inconspicuous toys, and beneath resting grandparents. I might hide eggs in places that are easy to see but challenging to get to. I might hide eggs in places that are the opposite of where they would expect to find them. I might lay a series of easy-to-find eggs that lead toward one that is very difficult to find. Whatever I do, I hide the eggs so my children will feel smart and capable when they find them. I give clues readily, but I keep them obscure at first so I can protect as much of that sensation of discovery, intelligence, and capability that comes from discovering something hidden as I can.

God is inviting us into the revelation of His nature. Again, we are finite beings in relationship with an infinite God. The journey of revelation may feel arduous or even cruel when we are feeling disconnected and discouraged, but this is an area where we have the opportunity to extend our trust toward our heavenly Father. If we believe He is hiding from us, then the process of revelation feels like a wild-goose chase. If we believe He is hiding for us, then it is a journey of adventure, discovery, and deepest intimacy.

The revelations we receive from seeing in the spirit, along with every other source, are intended to familiarize our hearts and minds with the nature of God. If we do not let the revelations we receive transform our hearts and minds, then there is no reason for God to give us further revelation—not because He is petulant or stingy but because we would almost certainly be unable to receive that revelation, even if it was right in front of us, because God reveals Himself to us layer upon layer, precept upon precept, and from glory to glory. If we miss a piece of who He is, we are ill-equipped to receive more of who He is.

Seeing Healing

I entered my first year at the Bethel School of Supernatural Ministry skeptical about all the testimonies of physical healing I heard come out of the school and church there in Redding, California. A few people were healed in the church where I grew up, maybe one or two a year, but the people at Bethel were reporting dozens of healing testimonies every week, sometimes more. I just couldn't see God healing that many people.

We prayed for healing fairly often at my church, once or twice a month at least. I would see things happen in the spirit when people prayed—things always happen when people do—but I could never see them very clearly. Once we were praying for someone who was about to have back surgery. As people surrounded the person who stood for prayer, I saw about six or seven angels circle around them. The angels had golden wings on their backs, were wearing silver-colored robes, and were each holding something in their hand. No matter how I squinted or tilted my head, I could not get the objects in their hands to come into focus. I could see every detail of the golden feathers that made up their wings, but the objects in their hands looked blurry and indistinct, as if someone had rubbed grease over those parts of the image. All I could tell was each angel looked as if it were holding the same thing and each object was roughly the size of a baseball bat.

Whatever the objects were, each angel extended its object forward as the people began praying for the man. The whole image went blurry for a moment as they prayed, and then the man began jumping up and down, declaring the pain had all gone. I found out later he had been able to cancel the surgery.

Another time, a group of about ten people went up to

the front of the church for prayer regarding several different illnesses. As the whole congregation prayed, I saw a blurry smear of iridescent light swoosh back and forth across the line of people. As before, with the objects in the angels' hands, no matter what I did, I could not see the light any clearer. Afterward only one person reported any change in his or her condition.

It ended up being like that most of the time we prayed for people to be healed—one out of every ten would get healed, maybe fewer, maybe more. And I usually couldn't see what was happening in the spirit very well regardless of the end result.

Healing seemed like a delicate thing to me, as if you had to get everything just right. If someone—the person who was sick or one of the people praying—was lacking faith or had some secret sin, then it just wouldn't work. If you prayed too loudly or too quietly, or too short or too long, it wouldn't work. If it was not the right time or the right place, or if the person praying just did not have the gift of healing, it wouldn't work. God wanted to heal—of course He did; what good God wouldn't—but healing was a delicate thing usually messed up by imperfect people. That's what I thought anyway, but this picture of healing was completely shattered when a friend of mine was diagnosed with leukemia.

He was young, just a few years older than me, and the disease hit him hard. He was in and out of the hospital for months, on the verge of death one day, then on the mend the next. Despite the dramatic swings in his health, he maintained an incredibly positive attitude and a remarkable devotion to the Lord. He trusted God completely, was devoted to Him fully, and spent nearly every one of his waking hours pursuing Him. Apart from this, my friend was just kind; he was thoughtful and friendly, courteous and genuine. He did not hide his suffering but was not above being humorous about his plight either. He was good. I cannot find a better way to say it. He was not perfect, of course—none of us are—but he was good.

The whole church prayed for him relentlessly, other churches prayed for him regularly, and I prayed for him too. I saw angels surrounding him—never fewer than six or seven—every time I visited him in the hospital. They wiped his head with cloths dipped in oil, flapped their wings over the machines cleaning impurities from his blood, and danced as he played worship music during his treatments.

I could not imagine him not being healed. I was surprised it was taking so long. I guessed God must be waiting for a particularly dramatic or beautiful moment to heal my friend—when at least a few hundred people would get saved all at once. Maybe his suffering would lead to some greater purpose or build to some more meaningful crescendo.

His family and mine went camping one summer when my friend was doing a bit better than usual. He told me for the first time that he had always wanted to see angels and asked me if I would pray for him to receive the gift of seeing in the spirit. I stood behind him as we sat around the campfire, laying my hands on his shoulders. I prayed a simple prayer. I only ever pray until I see the impartation land.

Immediately my friend saw a pair of tree-sized arms reach down from heaven, carrying a golden bowl full of oil and spices. It poured the mixture over him, covering him completely from head to toe with a tingling warmth. He saw angels ascending and descending all around our campsite as we worshipped together that night. He saw angels every day for the rest of his life, which I am sad to say lasted only a few weeks longer. His father told me later that he was singing worship songs and talking about the angels he saw as the ambulance rushed him to the hospital on the last day of his life. He was good.

Our whole church was shocked and heartbroken, the other churches that had been praying for him were shocked and heartbroken, and I was shocked and heartbroken. Sure, I believed that healing was delicate. I thought things had to be just right, that the person had to be just right. The problem was, I couldn't think of anyone more deserving of healing than my friend. He had faith that inspired me every time I was in the same room as him. He had joy that soared well beyond his circumstances. He was committed to God in a way that challenged me to give even more of my life over to Him. Surely he deserved to be healed.

Maybe not everyone who prayed for him had his or her heart in the right place, but there were so many people who were contending to see him healed. At least some of them had to be operating from genuine faith. If my friend had done nothing to make him undeserving of healing, and there were people full of faith contending for that healing, then why had he not been healed? Why did he die? I believed that God was good—I had already seen too much of His nature to let even this pain shake my belief in that—but still my friend was dead.

My only conclusion was that God must have had some greater purpose for my friend's sickness and death, that this tragedy would lead to some otherwise unobtainable good, that maybe my friend had somehow even agreed to this assignment, that he was sitting up in heaven looking down on us with the satisfaction that he had made way for God's plans.

If I could no longer blame the character of others for the lack of healing, then it must be that God, in certain cases, used sickness to accomplish His good works. That must be it, right?

The Key

Because of this I started my first year at Bethel, a place famous for its healing testimonies, with a certain amount of skepticism. Why would God be healing so many people? Wouldn't that undermine the purposes He had for that sickness?

It was not long before I realized the people at Bethel had a very different view on healing than I did. Teacher after teacher spoke about how it was always God's will to heal, saying that He did not use sickness to achieve His plans and that healing was meant to be a normal part of the Christian life. Appealing as these ideas were, I could not find a way to reconcile them with my experience. If God always wanted to heal, then why hadn't my friend been healed? I suppose my friend could have had some secret sin or some deeply hidden lack of faith, but I had seen no sign of these things. Moreover, the idea that he had done anything to prevent his healing simply did not ring true.

As I continued to hear testimonies and teaching about healing at Bethel, my hope began to grow. Maybe, just maybe, despite what experience had taught me, healing was more available than I thought. In the Bible every person who came to Jesus left completely healed. I could try to make the excuse that this was only because He was the Son of God, but that was not consistent with His commandments to His disciples and followers. Jesus commanded His disciples to heal the sick and promised they would do even greater things than they saw Him do. Revelation by revelation, I began to feel my hope continue to grow.

After a few months at school the rest of the students and I were released to minister on the prayer line after services on Sunday. I walked to the front of the church, feeling both nervous and excited. There were at least twenty students lining the front of the church, ready to pray for any who came to receive it. After only a few seconds someone approached me for prayer.

He told me he had severe pain in his back. He had been dealing with the pain for several months and was beginning to grow concerned that it was something serious. I reached out my hand and placed it on his shoulder and began to pray. At first I prayed a generic prayer: "Back, be healed in Jesus' name."

Nothing happened.

"I release the healing oil of heaven to run down his back."

Still nothing.

I tried filling my voice with a little more authority, "I command his body to come into alignment with heaven. I command all pain to go."

Again, nothing.

Not sure of what else to pray, I stayed silent, making sure to scrunch up my face so it looked like I was concentrating rather than panicking. All the fears and doubts that plagued my thoughts after my friend passed away came drifting back up to the surface of my mind: God does not want to heal everyone. Healing is tricky and precise. There is probably something wrong with you or your prayer.

A gentle whisper spoke over the sound of my compiling thoughts, "Why aren't you looking in the spirit?"

A cold fear gripped at my chest. Dozens of memories of all the times I saw angels around my friend during his extended illness came rushing through my mind. I was reminded of all the little beacons of hope I felt upon seeing the presence of angelic helpers in my friend's time of need and of the feeling I had as every one of those hopes crumbled to pieces when he died.

Even in this comparatively minor situation, praying for someone I hardly knew for a problem that was well below life-threatening, I felt scared to have my hopes dashed again. Some deep part of me knew, however, that refusing to find the courage to try again, to believe again, would be choosing to leave those fragments of broken hope at the bottom of my heart. Protecting my heart from being hurt would only preserve the hopelessness I held there. The only way to heal hope deferred is by taking the risk of hoping again.

I looked in the spirit. An angel stood on the opposite side of the man, resting a hand on his shoulder. I immediately recognized it as his personal angel. Its eyes were closed in prayer, but it opened them briefly and gave me a quick smile, acknowledging and affirming my care for his person before returning to his prayer.

My eyes drifted downward to the man's back. Squinting, I saw a blurry patch between his shoulder blades. Another wave of frustration hit me. Everything having to do with healing was almost always blurry or abstract beyond usefulness. What was I supposed to do with a blurry patch?

"Ask a question," the Holy Spirit whispered.

I placed two fingers on the man's back and traced a circle around the blurry place. "Is this the spot where it hurts?"

"Yeah," he said. "That's the center of it. It kind of emanates from right there."

The moment he spoke, the blurry mass came into sharp relief. It was a small clamp about the size of my fist with multiple metal fingers that wrapped around his spine between his shoulder blades. Sticking out from the clamp was a simple, flat, metal key.

One of the fragments of hope at the bottom of my heart said, "Could it really be that easy?"

The voice of the Holy Spirit responded, "It could."

Feeling silly and not at all confident, I leaned over to the man and said, "I see a picture of a clamp with a key attached to this place on your spine. I'm going to go ahead and just do a prophetic act and turn this key."

After the man agreed, I reached up and placed my hand over the key. I felt only air under my fingers as I turned it.

"Lefty-loosey," I said to myself, reminded of the first time my dad taught me how to use a socket wrench. I cranked the key around three full revolutions, feeling nothing but seeing the key turn with the motion of my hand.

The man straightened up a little more with each twist. I leaned forward after the final turn and asked, "Do you feel anything?"

"Yes!" he said, turning around with a gleam of joy in his eye, "The tightness and pain in my back got looser, then looser, then looser, and now it's completely gone."

He bent this way and that, testing the former injury. "Yes!" he said again. "It's totally better." He thanked me and left, making room for the next person in line.

This person had a bad headache. She was healed after my first prayer.

The next person had injured her hand many years before and was still unable to close it completely. She was able to make a fist, give a thumbs-up, and move her hand freely after three minutes of prayer.

Revelation Establishes Truth

I saw a total of five people get healed that day. Since then I have seen dozens and dozens more. I have also seen dozens and dozens not get healed. But something changed that day when I faced my hopelessness. Ever since I decided to take the risk of believing it is always God's will to heal and found the courage to look for it in the spirit, I have found that I see His provision to heal every single time.

Since that day every time I have prayed for healing, I have seen the healing present. Every time I have seen someone else pray for healing, I have seen the healing present. It doesn't always show up the same way. Sometimes I see an angel carrying a bowl of healing into the room. Sometimes I see the healing dripping from my hands like thick, green oil. Sometimes I see it rushing through the whole room like a flood. Sometimes I see it as a fountain of fresh, clean water springing up out of the ground. But it is always there.

Though I see the healing there every time, I do not see it manifest in the person every time, or even most of the time. Sometimes it is clear why that happens. Sometimes the bitterness or unforgiveness is so thick in a person's heart that you don't even need to see in the spirit to recognize it is there.

I was praying for a woman once who was experiencing prickling pain throughout the nerves in her body and partial paralysis in her face. Her description of her malady included several asides about her husband, who had just run off with a woman half her age. As I prayed for the pain she was experiencing in her body, I saw an angel standing next to her with a pillar of green flame in its left hand. Each time I prayed, the angel extended its hand to place the fire in her chest, but as soon as the flame got within a few inches of her, it extinguished. When the angel pulled its hand back, the flame reignited, but when the angel reached out to touch her, the flame went out again. After the third attempt the angel began to weep.

I tried to broach the subject of forgiveness toward her husband, but as soon as I mentioned him, her expression grew stony.

"Why should I forgive him?" she said with her lips pursed in a tight line. "He is not sorry. He doesn't care. How can I even forgive something like that?"

At this the angel continued to weep, saying, "He would give you that too, if only you would take it."

She turned away and left before I could tell her that God was able to provide for something as impossible as forgiveness just as much as He was able to provide for something as impossible as healing.

Sometimes it is clear why someone is not being healed, but sometimes it is not clear at all. I was part of the ministry team at one healing meeting where I had already seen three people healed in a row. One of them was in a severe bus accident several years before and still had fragments of glass embedded in her face. As we prayed, fragments of glass began to fall into her hands and the puffiness, a remnant of doctors' attempts to repair the damage, began to disappear. By the time we were done, she looked like a completely different person.

After a miracle such as that one, I felt ready to take on just about anything. My heart felt swollen with faith. The next woman who came to me had been dealing with back pain for several years. After seeing such an incredible miracle just a few minutes before, praying felt like a mere formality for a problem so small. Yet no matter how we prayed, the woman's condition did not improve. An angel stood just behind the woman with healing oil dripping from its hands. I neither saw nor discerned anything blocking or preventing this woman from receiving her healing, and I felt more full of faith than I ever had in my life, but still she ended up walking away with the malady she came with.

I was at another meeting several years later, and it was going terribly. I had a pounding headache, most of the people were not paying attention while I taught, and just as the meeting was ready to close, I felt the presence of the Holy Spirit ready to release healing.

"Oh no," I thought, "I want this to be over. I want to go to sleep. This meeting was terrible. Please let it be over." But the presence of the Holy Spirit did not relent or retreat. Knowing I would regret ignoring His invitation more than not getting what I wanted, I invited my team to the front to pray for those dealing with pain or illness.

A man hobbled up to me wearing a thick and worn-out back brace. He was at least 350 pounds and smelled like stale beer. "I've been on disability for seventeen years," he said in a thick voice. "Pain pills don't even do anything anymore. I don't bother with them. Can't even bend over to look at my feet." He demonstrated, hunching his shoulders in a feeble attempt at bending forward. He cringed at the pain the effort caused him. "Almost keeled over the last time I bent to pick up the TV remote..."

"All right," I said, interrupting as he continued to add details to his story, "let's pray then."

My head still pounding with pain, my faith well below zero, I extended my hand toward his back and thought, "This ain't happening."

As my hand got within three inches of the man's back, he let out a loud shout.

"Whoa!" he yelled. "Wow! Holy moly!" He dove forward, touched his toes, and then whipped into a tremendous backbend. He leaned way over to one side and then the other.

"Wow, preacher. I felt heat shoot all down through my back. The pain is all gone. I haven't felt this way in seventeen years," he said, continuing to twist and turn in every direction. "What did you do?"

"Nothing," I said, my jaw hanging somewhere near the floor. "I definitely didn't do anything."

I do not know why some people are healed and some are not. Why would one person be healed when I had little or no faith and a bad attitude while another is not healed when much faith is present? Why was my friend not healed when he was surrounded by such hope and filled with such faith? I do not know all the answers to these questions. But ever since I had the courage to start believing it is God's desire that all should be healed, that Jesus paid for every healing with His sacrifice on the cross, I started seeing all the healing that was available.

Revelation Transforms

A foundational principle of growing and stewarding the gift of seeing in the spirit is the understanding that revelation transforms. When we see in the spirit, or receive revelation in any other form, it is intended to transform the way we think and act. The apostle Paul states in 1 Corinthians 14:3 that the gift of prophecy is intended for edification, exhortation, and comfort. We sometimes translate the word *edification* as "encouragement" or "building up." This is not entirely wrong, since I do believe that prophecy is intended to encourage us and build us up, but that is only one part of what the word *edification* means. The word translated "edification" means to build an edifice or building. It implies the building of a structure. Prophetic words and the revelations that come through them are intended to be bricks and mortar in our lives. They help us build up our identity in Christ and our understanding of His kingdom. They are not the structure itself in the same way that a brick is not a building and cement is not a foundation; they are elements that, when following the architectural plans of heaven, form together with other parts to become a manifestation of that design.

When I had a partial understanding of healing, I only saw part of it in the spirit. In one of the earlier examples I could see the angels that arrived to release healing, but I could not see the tools, or objects I assume were tools, they used to release the healing. In the next example I could not see more than an abstract representation of the healing that was present. Nor could I see why one person was healed while nine others were not. I could see the angels present to bring comfort and worship alongside my sick friend. I could even see angels that seemed to be part-nering with the doctors' attempt to keep him alive, but I could not see God's plan for healing for him.

It was not until I was in a culture that had a superior understanding of God's purpose for healing and until I chose to take the risk of believing God really did want to heal everyone that I was able to see the healing that was available around me.

This did not, of course, cause every person I have prayed for to be healed from that point forward. But it did allow me to see the truth that God is always ready to heal. From the moment I took the risk of looking at the man with pain in his back and partnering with the Holy Spirit to release healing by turning the metal key I saw, I have always seen healing come when it is asked for, 100 percent of the time.

The truth is that this has left me with more questions than answers. Why didn't my friend get healed? Is it my fault if I pray for someone who does not get healed? Or is it the person's fault? Is it anyone's fault at all? Or is it some other factor I have yet to consider? If healing is available every single time, then is the problem that we do not know how to access it? Is it that we don't know how to listen to the instructions God is giving us?

I still do not know why my friend was not healed, but knowing God's intention for healing helps me set my hopes and my heart in the right direction. It also makes it easier to resist the urge to come to a conclusion about the things I do not understand. My conclusions about healing prevented me from seeing what God was making available. But I have learned my lesson there. I will not allow myself to be satisfied by a conclusion that is not authored by His hand. To do less is to sell out my inheritance for short-term comfort.

I used the example of healing because it is a corner of God's kingdom that has been challenging for me in the past, but the principle of letting revelation transform us can be applied to just about anything. Every story in this book and the ones in my previous book are examples of revelation transforming my perspective. Look again, and you will see my perspective on worship, my beliefs about leaders in the church, my opinions about people who may seem strange at first glance, and my views on many other things change and grow because of the unfolding revelation of God's nature.

There are aspects of worship I could not see in the spirit

until I began to let the things I was already seeing transform the way I thought and acted during worship. There were aspects of prayer that were obscure and confusing to me until I started asking the Holy Spirit questions about His design for prayer. I could only see a small percentage of people's personal angels with any sort of clarity until I let the things I saw and the things God said lead me to grow a deep foundation of love for every person I met.

The gifts of the Spirit are not mere tools—they are models and expressions of God's nature, pictures and signs of who He is, and they work best when they function in alignment with the One who fashioned them. This goes well beyond having good character and strong morals and into partaking in the nature of God, which is impossible apart from the victory Jesus won on the cross.

If you want to see miracles, if you want to see people healed, if you want to see angels, if you want to see the dead raised, if you want to see people come into His kingdom by the thousands, if you want to see heaven on earth, then become a student of God's love. It is the foundation of His nature and the manifestation of His goodness.

SEEING-IN-THE-SPIRIT TRAINING— DAY 2,987

I CLENCHED BOTH HANDS ON the wheel as tightly as possible, fighting the wind as it threatened to push the medium-sized cargo truck into the next lane. I was part of a team driving down to do ministry in the northern part of Mexico, and somehow I had been chosen to drive the luggage truck. Another gust of wind caused the cab to rock back and forth as I fought to stay in my lane without overcorrecting and sliding into the ditch on the side of the road.

The trip was part of my first year at the Bethel School of Supernatural Ministry, a three-year school in Redding, California, focused on training people to continue in the ministry style Jesus modeled. Students learn how to hear the voice of God more clearly, release healing for the sick, discover deeper identity in Christ, and pursue worldwide transformation.

There were nearly three hundred of us driving down in a caravan of dozens of cars. To keep us together as much as possible, the leaders gave a walkie-talkie to each driver. Since most of the walkie-talkies were being held by passionate ministry school students, most of the airtime had been devoted to students giving prophetic words to people in the other cars. I had been ignoring them, mostly because I was devoting almost all my attention to not letting the wind blow the wobbly luggage truck into the side of a bridge embankment.

Just as the wind started to die down, a crackly voice called out my name over the radio: "Hey, Blake, this one is for you."

I immediately recognized the voice of one of my close friends, and at the same time, I felt a nervous energy shoot up my spine. My arms tensed, my muscles tightened, and every part of me readied itself as if I suddenly realized I was about to be hit by an oncoming freight train. I knew, even before she spoke, that the word my friend was about to give was going to change my life, and though what she said was simple, the grace God released through her words was the tipping point between one season of my history and another.

She said, "It's time to come out of the cave."

It had been nearly five years since I fully gave up on trying to share my gift of seeing. I shared a few things with a few people, but I could easily count those instances on my fingers. I still saw in the spirit everywhere I went every day. I still talked to the Holy Spirit about the things I saw. And the more I talked to Him, the more I saw.

Things were going well. I was comfortable. I felt more connected to God than I ever had. I felt for the first time that this gift could be used for something good. Seeing in the spirit made me feel closer to God. I had a small, nagging feeling of regret that I could not find a way to invite other people into the good I was experiencing, but I had already tried and failed enough. There just wasn't a way.

When the Holy Spirit told me to go to the Bethel School of Supernatural Ministry, I fought Him for months, knowing that going to a school like that would force me to share the things I saw. I was not ready for all the attention, questions, and pressure again. I was not ready to have so little of the glory in the things I saw make it into my descriptions again. I was not ready to fail again.

I fought Him for a whole year until finally I relented. Despite agreeing to go, I made a promise. "I'll go to this school of Yours," I said, "but I am not talking to anyone about seeing in the spirit. If You want me to deal with this, then You are going to have to make it happen."

I stuck to my promise, only telling a handful of people about the things I saw and insisting they not tell anyone else. I learned a lot and grew a lot, but I managed to keep my gift hidden for almost the entire school year—that is, until the end of the year, when all the students go out to different parts of the world for a mission trip.

"It's time to come out of the cave."

Those eight words echoed in my mind over and over again as I rattled and bumped my way down Interstate 5. It was not the most eloquent or detailed prophetic word I ever received, but every syllable carried a heat that still burned in the depths of my soul. They melted the elaborate defenses I had built around my gift, they cauterized the wounds I had experienced when trying to use my gift in the past, and they incinerated any attempt my mind made to deny the pure and simple truth: It was time to share this gift. It was time to start right away.

I started tentatively but immediately. As soon as I finished unloading my luggage at the facility in Mexico, I shared with a few of my bunkmates about what their personal angels looked like. We worshipped together as a team in a small chapel at the facility, and I shared what I saw with a few of the team members and leaders. I shared about the protection angels I saw with us when we went to minister in the slums. I shared about the worship angels I saw dancing around as students played music for a group of children.

Everything was going pretty well so far. I braced myself every time I opened my mouth to share what I was seeing, ready for the deluge of overwhelming questions and attention, but I was surprised at how gentle my fellow students' questions seemed. It wasn't nearly as overwhelming as I remembered it being just a few years before. I got bolder and bolder as the trip went on, feeling more confident and assertive about sharing what I saw. It all came to a culmination near the end of our time in Mexico when we visited a church in the mountains.

Since there were so many students on the trip, we split into smaller groups to visit some of the local churches. I was on a team of about ten that went to a small church in the mountains near Tijuana. Feeling emboldened by the series of small successes I had experienced so far, I decided I should look in the spirit on our way to the church so I could share the things I saw with those at the church when we ministered to them later that night.

I looked out my window as we drove through trash-strewn streets, past houses made of tarps and particleboard. Despite the desolation of poverty, I could not help but feel a sense of beauty. In the spirit I saw a river of crystalline water filled with millions of flakes of gold running down the valley. Immediately I knew, without having known a moment before, that it was the blood of Jesus. As I looked at how it swiftly ran, touching every person and home along the way, I felt God's intention and attention on the valley. He was here, and He had a purpose.

As we pulled up to the church, a simple square building made of gray cinder blocks, I saw that there was no roof on the place in the spirit. Angels moved freely, going up and down, as a golden light poured down from above, filling the building. "There's nothing between them and God," I thought. "There's no separation."

We walked into the building to meet the handful of translators helping us that evening. I saw two large angels inside, each around twenty feet tall, with one standing in front of each entrance to the sanctuary. They were wearing ornate, colorful robes and holding equally ornate weapons. They looked equal parts warrior and priest. I got the impression they were there to bless and protect people on their way in and on their way out.

After meeting with our translators, the team went out into the surrounding village to pray for people and invite them to the meeting later that night. I made note of the things I saw along the way, excited to share them with the church later.

A few hours later I was standing onstage. There were a little over a hundred people, and the night had already been a great success. Two people were healed of deafness, one woman was healed of blindness in one of her eyes, and several people received prophetic words of encouragement and hope. My nerves crackled. I was just going to share a few of the random things I saw around their church. How could that compare to people getting healed or getting specific words about their identity and destiny? Regardless, there was no backing down now since I already had the mic in my hand. I began to speak, hoping that at the very least what I had to share would be interesting.

I described how I saw the river of Jesus' blood running down the valley and how it touched every person along the way. I explained how their building had no roof on it in the spirit, that there was nothing separating them and God. I described the two angels standing near the entrances and how they were meant to bless people who were coming in and going out.

I noticed as I finished describing the angels that the translator had stopped translating. Feeling confused, I turned to find him doubled over, weeping. More confused, I turned and looked at the crowd and realized many of them were weeping as well. I looked back at the translator, at a loss for how to proceed.

"You don't understand," the translator said, catching a breath. "You don't understand. You don't understand."

"I don't understand," I agreed internally, shaking my head.

"You don't understand," he said again, raising a finger to point at me. "This man was sent by God."

My confusion only grew.

"I am the pastor at this church," the translator said. "This is my church. These are my people. Everything that you said—everything, word for word, is exactly what we've been praying. We prayed that the blood of Jesus would flow through this valley. We asked God to send powerful angels to guard our doors. We prayed that our church would be fully open to heaven. You don't understand."

He turned to translate everything he had just said into Spanish, pausing frequently as waves of tears overtook him.

I stood, stunned and silent. I could not fathom why the things I shared had affected the congregation and the pastor so severely. I looked around the room at all the things I hadn't shared about. I saw a half dozen healing angels, each wearing a deep-green cloak and carrying a stone basin full of glowing, green water. I saw dozens of multicolored banners hanging from the walls, each unique in pattern and style. I saw worship angels hang up the banners they had been waving during worship with the others on the walls, each being placed like a trophy or plaque. I saw a dozen more angels moving throughout the room, breaking bad things off people, depositing good things in others. I saw the presence of God moving through the room like a silver and gold cloud, sweeping and weaving, looking for places and people it could inhabit more fully. Even all this was only a tenth of what was happening in that room at that moment. Why would the few casual observations I made be impressive or impactful? Why wouldn't they assume everything they prayed for had happened?

Then I heard the Holy Spirit speak. He said, "I have been renewing your mind," and suddenly it all made sense.

I had been so frustrated when I tried to share the things I saw. I experienced nothing but half successes and failures. I could not figure out how to use the gift God had given me to serve Him. In that moment I realized His first goal was not to give me a gift so I could serve Him—it was to give me a gift so I could know Him.

For more than eight years I had practiced seeing in the spirit. I saw thousands of angels, spiritual activity in hundreds of worship services, and dozens and dozens of other examples of His manifest presence. Each was a snapshot of His infinite goodness, kindness, and grace. Each of those snapshots, bit by bit, had completely transformed the way I saw the world—not just the way I saw it with my eyes but the way I saw it in my heart and the way it filtered through my mind.

The idea that it would be a huge revelation to the pastor that the things he and his congregation had been praying for had happened was foreign to me—not because I am so holy, full of faith, or anything like that but because I had already seen how heaven responded to ten thousand other prayers. It made as much sense as gravity. I don't have to have faith that a ball will drop if I let go of it. I have seen it happen ten thousand times; it is just how the world works.

I thought back to all the times I experienced frustration or disappointment when trying to share with others the things I saw. Sometimes it was hard because I did not know how to explain or describe the things I saw, and sometimes it was hard because I got more attention than I was comfortable with when I shared, but it was always hard because I never saw the beauty and grace I experienced when I saw heavenly things reflected in the eyes of the people I was sharing with. Though I did not fully understand what that beauty and that grace were or where they came from, when they were not released when I shared what I saw, it felt fundamentally wrong.

I realized as I stood on that stage in Mexico that the beauty and grace I felt in every good thing I saw was the reflected glory of God, His nature manifested in His creation. I realized the reason I could not release that glory when I spoke about the things I saw was not because I lacked eloquence or courage but because I had not yet grown familiar enough with His nature to represent it.

I had struggled, convinced my gift was for the benefit of others. The truth was that the first goal of the gift was to lead me to know the Giver. That is the only way I could be equipped to use it for the benefit of anyone. It was only then, at the tipping point between one season and the next, that I could see how I had been struggling to bear fruit when the only goal was to grow.

I went home from that trip knowing the time to start bearing fruit had come. I immediately asked a friend if I could speak at her home group. There I shared my full testimony for the first time. I talked about how I saw things when I was a kid. I talked about how I struggled to talk about the things I saw as a teenager. People started asking questions as soon as I finished sharing my story. The answers came more easily than they ever had before. Simple examples and illustrations came readily and without much effort. Soon, however, there were eight or nine hands shooting up as soon as the opportunity to ask another question came. I started to feel the overwhelming weight of people's expectations, and with it came the old fears.

As the anxiety began to claw its way up my throat, the Holy Spirit spoke firmly and clearly, "They are not hungry for you. They are hungry for Me."

All the weight that had started piling on my shoulders completely vaporized. This wasn't about satisfying people's expectations, giving people something interesting to talk about, or even telling people about angels; this was about revealing His nature. That was something I could give my time and energy to. If this gift was not just about the cool things I saw but about people having the opportunity to know God more, then that was something I could give my life for.

I knew I still had a lot of growing to do. I wanted to make sure that when I talked about seeing in the spirit, it wasn't just about how interesting or dynamic the things I saw were but about how everything always pointed back to God, His nature, and the opportunity we have to experience an intimate relationship with Him.

I always did my best to make this truth shine through as I began to travel and teach about seeing in the spirit around the world. It was never too hard because everything naturally pointed back to Him, but part of me always felt that there was a more profound way to illustrate how everything so perfectly tied back to connection with Him, a clearer way to show just how much He desired an intimate relationship with His children.

Maybe it was something I had yet to discover or see.

PART III

Heaven on Earth

GOD DOES NOT GIVE US spiritual gifts to make us more effective servants. He gives spiritual gifts to make us closer sons and daughters. True, good sons and daughters will be servants to their parents, but the context and heart behind their service are completely different from those of one who is serving for compensation or to fulfill an obligation. God's gifts exist to reveal His nature to us and through us. That is how we fulfill the Lord's Prayer and see His will done on earth as it is in heaven.

So how do I grow in these gifts? How do I know which gifts I have? What does it actually mean to bring heaven to earth? What does it actually mean to be God's son or daughter?

In the following section you will find one story. It is the best and, ultimately, only answer I have to these questions and every other question posed in this book. Look for how God reveals His nature. Think about what it means for you as God's adopted son or daughter if everything He says about Himself is true.

FACE TO FACE

IT WAS A TYPICAL SUNDAY morning church service. I was asked to run some of the audiovisual equipment because the person scheduled to do it was sick. I arrived early and made my way to the small room in the back corner of the sanctuary where all the video equipment was housed. I made sure my portion of the equipment was working properly and then popped my head out of the video room to make sure all the other preparations were going as planned.

Band members were tuning instruments, audio engineers were running cables and testing microphones, and worship angels were running through the steps of their celestial choreography. Everything looked completely normal. Then I noticed another angel sitting in a chair just a few feet from where I stood at the door to the video room.

This angel wore a dark-blue suit, though it was of a cut and style different from any I had ever seen. He sat, arms crossed, legs crossed, looking at the band members as they prepared for worship. His eyes looked sharp, and his posture was pristine, but I would have classified the expression on his face somewhere between mild disdain and boredom. Everything about him—the cut of his hair, the style of his suit, the measured way his eyes took in the room—reminded me of a jaded police detective. I knew this impression was just my mind trying to justify the familiarity my spirit felt when I saw the angel, so he was probably not a literal detective, but the general idea couldn't be too far off.

Something about the inquisitive glint in his eye, combined with the general impression of boredom I got from his bearing, made me think that he had come here looking for something, something that he did not expect to find.

I felt a surge of pride for my church rise in my chest. "We'll see about that," I said out loud, confident we would have anything and everything this angel was looking for, and turned back to my equipment.

People started arriving for the early service a few minutes later, and before long it was time for worship to start. Angels danced, people sang, and the band played; the detective angel didn't move. Worship ended, announcements were made, testimonies were shared, and the offering was taken; still the angel did not move.

Steve Hale, our senior leader, preached a message about worship, sharing about the value of bringing our best and giving our all when we come together to worship the King of kings. Still the angel remained seated in complete nonchalance.

"What could he be looking for?" I thought. A dozen angels had danced all around the room during worship, carrying long trains of multicolored silk that trailed behind them as they darted among the crowd of worshipping people. Three worship angels stood behind Steve as he spoke, releasing an impartation of worship in waves of liquid light. What was missing?

At the end of his talk, Steve invited the worship team to come back onstage to play one more song. He invited the congregation to come as close to the stage as possible and, in accordance with the message he shared, do their best to give their all to God in worship.

The first note the band played had all the momentum the last note had during worship. Worship has an ebb and flow. It is a call and response. We call out to God. God calls out to us. We come closer. He comes closer. There is a momentum built in this process, but it usually takes time to build, like getting reacquainted with a friend you haven't seen in a while. You might shake hands before going in for a polite hug and have a few cliché "How have you been? Just fine. You?" kind of lines before your conversation takes on the comfort and openness found in the familiarity of friendship.

The last song felt more like the moment when you and your friend run to meet each other and collide into a full-armed embrace. The band dove straight into the chorus, and those in the crowd immediately started jumping, dancing, and raising their hands. The presence of God rushed into the room like a thick, white cloud, making the air vibrate with electric life. As soon as the music started, the detective angel immediately uncrossed his arms and legs and leaned forward, a look of shocked anticipation on his face. This made me take a few steps out of the video room to get a better look at what was happening in the sanctuary.

The cloud continued to flow into the room, spreading out to fill every corner, but it remained most concentrated around the tight crowd pressing closer and closer to the stage. There it grew thicker and thicker until I had to squint to see the stage through it. Then all at once, at six or seven different places around the stage, the cloud tightened, twisted, and condensed into a single point, creating a tiny bead of iridescent blue light. Each was no bigger than a pea.

The detective angel stood up the moment the beads of light appeared, and he began walking forward, brisk but calm. As he walked, he reached into his coat pocket and pulled out a set of mechanical golden tweezers and a small leather pouch. It was not until the angel got close to the front that I realized the beads of light were not floating in the air—they were sitting inside people's hearts. The cloud was so thick and the beads so bright that I hadn't noticed.

The angel reached into each person as if his or her skin were no more substantial than smoke, and with the precision and deftness of a master surgeon he used the tweezers to extract the blue beads, placing each in his leather bag. Soon he had collected them all.

He paused for a moment, lifting his head as if he were trying to catch a scent, and then moved to a woman standing on the far side of the room. I could not see any sign of a glowing bead in her heart, but the angel began poking and prodding at her chest with his golden tweezers. After a few seconds I saw a quick flash of blue light as the angel pulled a bead from somewhere deep in her chest and placed it in his bag.

He repeated this process a few more times with two or three more people, extracting beads of light, none of which I could see until he pulled them free. After this the angel lifted his head, scanned the crowd one more time, returned the pouch to his coat pocket, walked back to his seat, sat down, and returned to his indifferent posture—arms crossed, legs crossed.

The song continued for a few more minutes. No more of the blue beads showed up, but the cloud remained even after people started to walk back to their seats to retrieve their things on the way out.

I stared at the detective angel, my lips pressed together in thought. What were those beads? And why did they only show up at the end?

The angel turned, looked me up and down, then returned his gaze to the front of the room and said, "I have been looking everywhere for this kind of praise. It is extremely rare, delicate, and easy to miss, but it is precious to the Father."

After receiving no further comment from the angel, I returned to the video room, excited to see what would happen during the second service.

~

At first the second service went the same. People and angels all danced together during worship while the detective angel remained seated in composed indifference. We continued with announcements, testimonies, and the offering, all without any change in the angel's demeanor. Again, Steve shared his message about worship, and again, he invited the congregation to gather in front of the stage for one more song.

It was as if the people in the second service were trying to outdo the people in the first service. The momentum of worship returned instantly; the thick, white cloud filled the room immediately; and more than twenty of the beads of light appeared within the first few seconds of worship. I stepped all the way out of the video room to get a good look as the detective angel got up to go collect the beads, and I froze in my tracks as, without any warning, the face of God emerged from the back wall behind the stage and came into the room.

It came so suddenly, so clearly, and so unexpectedly that without thinking, I screamed, ran into the video room, and slammed the door shut behind me.

A strange mixture of terror and elation swam up and down my body. That was wrong. That was not biblical. No one is supposed to see that. Doubts and fears boiled up from all directions. I had always been taught that we cannot see God's face, and every scripture and teaching that supported this fact began rushing through my head in a near panic. That was Him. He is good. He is a good Father. Truths about His nature calmed the fears as quickly as they came, though they did not stop coming. Every teaching and scripture about His goodness and love flooded through my heart, reminding me of the intimacy of my lifelong relationship with Him.

These two schools of thought slammed together in my head, holding massive debates and forming detailed arguments a dozen times a second. He is too big, too holy, and we are too small, too simple. I shouldn't have seen that. He is good, He is kind, He closed the gap, and He sent His Son to do it. Maybe I could see Him if He let me.

Overwhelmed with colliding thoughts and emotion, I continued arguing with myself.

"You just saw that!"

"No, I didn't."

"You know you did. You couldn't deny it if you wanted to."

"That's impossible."

"Of course it is."

"Apparently not."

"I'm not supposed to see that!"

"Why not?"

"Because I'm not allowed to."

"It wasn't my fault. I didn't try to see it."

"Maybe it wasn't what I thought."

"You know what it was."

Parts of me tried desperately to minimize or deny what I had seen. But the sheer reality of His face burned in the folds of my mind, refusing to be pushed anywhere but further to the front of my thoughts.

"You should go back out there."

"No, I should not."

"You'll regret it if you don't."

"I can't."

"You're regretting not being out there already."

This continued for somewhere between ten seconds and two hours until, trembling, my hands balled into fists, I pushed the door open, and I walked back out into the sanctuary. And there He was again, as clear and real and undeniably God as He had been when He first came.

I looked at Him for two seconds, then looked at the ground. I regretted every millisecond I spent doing that, so I looked up. It was too overwhelming, too intense, so I looked down again. Back and forth my gaze went, ping-ponging between His face and the carpet, until I stopped and stayed staring at the ground. I couldn't. I just couldn't, and I didn't know why.

Dozens of scriptures, hundreds of thoughts, and millions of emotions ran through my mind, swarming and bumping around before I could latch onto any one of them. Then the voice of God came so clearly and loudly that it wiped every thought out of my mind, silencing every synapse, leaving room only for His words.

He said, "Who told you that you should *ever* hide your face from Mine?"

Immediately a memory flashed up on the projection screen of my mind. I was four years old, sitting in my Sunday school class. The church met in a high school gymnasium, and the kids' classes were held in small classrooms made of rolling modular walls. I was sitting at the far left in the third row. A little girl in the front row on the right raised her hand to ask a question.

"Teacher, but why can't we see God?"

The woman at the front of the room paused for a moment, considering the question, then answered, "Oh, honey, God is just so big and powerful, if we ever saw Him, we couldn't handle it—we would die."

The memory was gone as quick as it had come, but it told me what I needed to know—at least for the moment. I didn't know if I was allowed to see God's face. I didn't know if what I was doing was theologically correct. But what I did know was that it was not God who told me I could not see His face—it was a person. With that little scrap of permission held tightly in my heart, I lifted my eyes and stared full into His face.

It was the most familiar thing I had ever seen in my entire life. And though His face was so big it filled the whole front part of the room, He looked like a person. He had a nose, a mouth, two eyes, two ears, and hair. I could see a resemblance to every person I ever knew or met, yet He didn't look exactly like any of them. Every feature, gesture, and movement echoed every touch of His presence I had felt throughout my history with Him. I couldn't measure the kindness in His eyes, the care He showed with every glance. He made eye contact with each person, one at a time, not hurrying, taking just the right amount of time for each one. He leaned forward and rubbed His face on all the people gathered at the front of the stage as if they were a warm blanket. Every single thing about Him confirmed and superseded my greatest hopes for His goodness, kindness, and glory. I stared at Him for the rest of the song, stretching my eyes as far open as they would go, desperate to take in every single part.

Eventually the song ended, and, letting out a deep, satisfied sigh, He backed out of the room the same way He came in. I shuffled back into the video room, slumped into a corner, and let tears run down my cheeks. No thoughts came. No opinions. Instead, I just basked in the glow of His goodness.

Thoughts to Ponder

- We will be moving on to how I unpacked this experience, both biblically and personally, in the following chapter, but before we do that, take a moment to take stock of what your heart is saying and doing. How did hearing that story make you feel? Did it scare you or fill you with hope? Did it cause anger or release peace?

- Why do you think you responded to that story the way you did?

ACTIVATION AND STUDY—
INTENT

IN THE PAST WHEN I experienced similarly dramatic and life-altering visions or encounters, I usually kept them to myself for a long time. I tend to process things slowly. I do not want to be too hasty to draw conclusions about the things I see. After three or four years I might share one of these intense visions with my close friends or family. Then, after another three or four years, I would start to feel the Holy Spirit asking me to share my experience publicly. I would usually get around to actually sharing it a year or two after that. I prefer to let my experiences mature before I share them with others.

Knowing this, you can understand my dismay when just six months after the experience I described in the previous chapter, the Holy Spirit asked me to share the story. I was at the Bethel Atlanta School of Supernatural Ministry retreat, a fun trip to the beach we use to kick off the new school year with our students and staff.

The retreat sets the pace and tone for what God is going to be releasing that year to the students, so I always make sure I am flowing with what the Holy Spirit wants me to teach during the retreat. I rarely know what I am going to talk about more than a day before I teach when I am there. This is not my norm when traveling or teaching at our church on Sunday, but I had been going to the Bethel Atlanta School of Supernatural Ministry retreat for long enough that I had grown comfortable with the divergence from my normal teaching routine.

It was the night I was assigned to teach, and I had no idea what I was supposed to share. We were two songs into worship, I was going to be speaking in less than twenty minutes, and I still did not know what I was going to talk about. The Holy Spirit came to my aid just as the third song was wrapping up.

"I want you to tell *that* story."

"*That* story?" I responded, knowing exactly which story He meant. "I can't tell *that* story."

"Yes, you can."

"No, I can't. I haven't figured it out. I don't even know if that was OK. How can I share that with a bunch of first-year students?"

"You can because I told you to."

Panic set in as I realized I was losing the argument. I could go up with nothing, but that would just be trading one kind of disaster for another. It may seem like nothing to you, but sharing a story such as that one without a great deal of processing and conversation with the Holy Spirit was miles beyond my normal realm of comfort.

"Fine," I said, "if You want me to share the story, then You have to give me something. Just give me a scripture, anything."

Immediately the Holy Spirit said, "Exodus 33."

I turned there and started reading. It turned out to be one of my favorite pieces of biblical history—Moses and

God in the tent of meeting, discussing the nature of God's relationship with man. A part near the end caught my eye:

> Then Moses said, "Now show me your glory."
> And the LORD said, "I will cause all my goodness to pass in front of you, and I will proclaim my name, the LORD, in your presence. I will have mercy on whom I will have mercy, and I will have compassion on whom I will have compassion. But," he said, "you cannot see my face, for no one may see me and live."
> —EXODUS 33:18–20

"Yeah," I said, making no attempt to hide the frustration in my voice, "that's exactly what I'm talking about. I don't know if I was even allowed to see that. I don't even know why I saw what I did."

"Galatians 2:20," the Holy Spirit said, cutting me off.

So I turned there:

> I have been crucified with Christ and I no longer live, but Christ lives in me. The life I now live in the body, I live by faith in the Son of God, who loved me and gave himself for me.
> —GALATIANS 2:20

And then it hit me. I had always been told we could not see God because He was too big, too powerful, or too holy and we were too sinful, too imperfect, or too lowly to see Him face to face. All the scriptures about being born again ran through my mind.

Therefore if anyone is in Christ, he is a new creature; the old things passed away; behold, new things have come.

—2 CORINTHIANS 5:17, NASB

Blessed be the God and Father of our Lord Jesus Christ, who according to His great mercy has caused us to be born again to a living hope through the resurrection of Jesus Christ from the dead.

—1 PETER 1:3, NASB

Or do you not know that all of us who have been baptized into Christ Jesus have been baptized into His death?

—ROMANS 6:3, NASB

God did not ignore the stipulation He gave Moses in Exodus 33, "No one may see me and live." He fulfilled it. He made death and rebirth part of the process of salvation.

Profound Good

I could feel the very foundation of my perception of the gospel rattling underneath my feet. I flashed back to the story of the fall of man. Whenever I picture that story, I always remember an old children's Bible story cartoon series I used to watch as a kid.

I remembered the frightening music that played when Adam and Eve ate the forbidden fruit. As Adam bit into the fruit, the sky grew dark. Thunder began to sound, and lightning parted the sky. The voice of God came in a stern, echoing baritone, "Adam, where are you?"

Suddenly I realized how incongruous that image was

with the God I know. I could feel how false that version of the story was, so I flipped back to the Book of Genesis to look at the story more closely. I breezed through the familiar passages, reading about how the serpent deceived Adam and Eve into eating the forbidden fruit. Then I ran into something that jumped out at me. They ate the fruit, their eyes were opened, and they made clothes from fig leaves, but:

> Then they heard the sound of the LORD God walking in the garden in the cool of the day, and the man and his wife hid themselves from the presence of the LORD God among the trees of the garden.
> —GENESIS 3:8, MEV

As I read this verse, I realized something I had never considered in the context of this story. God, being all knowing, probably knew what they had done, right? That means God's first response to original sin was not to appear in a cloud of thunder and rage—it was to go for a walk and talk about it. God's first act in response to original sin was an act of intimacy and relationship. It was man who hid from God, not God who hid from man. Yes, mankind had violated the terms of the relationship. Yes, that violation caused separation between man and God. But God's first response was one of connection.

As I came to terms with this subtly, but profoundly, altered perspective on the fall of man, my instinct told me to take a closer look at the restoration of man. I flipped forward to the Book of Matthew and landed near the moment of Jesus' death. There I found something that finally brought my shifting foundation to rest. To contextualize it properly, however, I have to give you a little background.

In the time between the fall of man and the death of Jesus, a method of God relating to man and man relating to God was established. The fine points of this arrangement were laid out between God and Moses and can be found in detail in the first five books of the Bible. One of the specifics of this covenant that always stuck out to me was in a design element of the tabernacle and later the temple, the place where God's presence dwelled among His people.

In the temple and tabernacle was a room called the holy of holies or the most holy place. This was the most sacred place. It was where the ark of the covenant was kept; it was where God's presence rested. This place was separated from the rest of the tabernacle or temple by a thick veil, a curtain. It was considered dangerous to go into that place; in fact, the Israelites believed if someone entered the most holy place under the wrong conditions, he would drop dead, unable to survive in the direct presence of God. It was a sign of the separation and the distance between God and man.

With that in mind, let's look at the moment of Jesus' death:

> And Jesus, when He had cried out again with a loud voice, released His spirit. At that moment the curtain of the temple was torn in two, from the top to the bottom. And the ground shook, and the rocks split apart.
>
> —MATTHEW 27:50–51, MEV

That curtain was the veil between the most holy place and the rest of the temple. The moment Jesus died, it was ripped in two. I had read that scripture at least a hundred times, but in light of my recent experience it took on a completely different context.

The veil was torn the moment Jesus died. The very moment. Taking a step back and looking at the whole picture, it almost doesn't make sense. Why wasn't the veil torn three days later when Jesus was raised from the dead or even later when He ascended into heaven? Why was it torn the moment Jesus died?

The only image I can find to make sense of this is one of a God so desperate to be reunited with His people that He was pressing against the separation between Himself and mankind, waiting for the moment He could burst forth and be present with His children once more. The torn veil speaks not of an angry Lord annoyed at the effort needed to correct the mistakes of His servants but of a loving Father, desperate to be reunited with His treasured children.

God's intent, from the beginning to now and for all time, is to be with His people. Adam and Eve recognized the sound of God coming to walk with them. That means it was a familiar sound, one they could recognize at a distance. It was normal for Him to come walk with them. The veil in the temple was torn at the moment of Jesus' death. The Father did not wait a moment longer than was needed to claim what He had paid for.

This is it, my friends—this is *the* profound good. This is the crux of the gospel, the purpose behind every spiritual gift, and the culmination and motivation of every plan of heaven. We have a God who chose to have a relationship with us.

It is impossible to see God. It is impossible to know

God. He is too big, too holy, and too powerful. It is impossible to relate to God—that is, unless He wants us to.

What we believe is so important. If we believe in an angry God, then we will see Him. If we believe in a disappointed God, then we will see Him. If we believe in a distant God, then we will see Him. But if we dare to believe in a God who loves us truly and well, then we will see Him. What we believe about God's intent toward us is the filter that determines what aspects of His nature we will and will not experience.

We have been fed a lie, a thousand times in a thousand different ways. We have been fed the lie that it was or is God's intention to separate Himself from us. This lie is justified by our mistakes and inadequacies, reinforced by our wounds, and propped up by life experiences that, if looked at in a certain way, are evidence of a distant God. But if you dare to believe what God says about Himself is true, if you have the courage to hope Paul was declaring the truth when he said we have been crucified with Christ, then you will begin to see the God of love has been with you every day of your life.

Almost a year went by before I realized why God's face looked so familiar to me that day at the back of the church. It was because I had already seen it—a hundred thousand times, a million times, reflected in every angel I saw, present in moments of connection and love with my family, close through the trials and trouble I faced, woven throughout my hopes and dreams for the future, there in my greatest victories and my greatest defeats, and with me since before I took in my first breath on the day I was born.

I had been seeing His face my whole life. That Sunday was just the first time I saw it with my eyes.

Continuing to Grow

Many people miss that God is always inviting us to know Him more, which is why many do not continue to grow in the gift of seeing in the spirit. If you see something large and dramatic, such as a twenty-foot-tall angel with a fiery sword, then it is an invitation to know God more. If you see a little streak of light out of the corner of your eye, then it is an invitation to know God more. If you see nothing, if you feel you cannot hear His voice at all, then it is an invitation to know God more. He is always inviting you in.

Everyone hits obstacles and plateaus while growing in the gift of seeing in the spirit, including me. It is how we decide to engage during these seasons that determines what happens next.

Maybe you have experienced obstacles right out of the gate. Maybe you are not seeing anything or sensing anything, and you do not know how to learn to trust what you are seeing in your mind's eye. Maybe you have started seeing, but most of the things you see come only as imprints upon your imagination. Maybe you are seeing things with your eyes, but they are often obscure, abstract, or too brief to derive any meaning from them. Whatever your obstacle or plateau looks like, here are a few keys to get you jump-started.

Research and dig.

This is a wonderful thing to do if you feel as if you cannot see anything at all or if you are feeling very uncertain about the images you see in your mind's eye. Find more books about the gift of seeing in the spirit and more people who are teaching it. Jonathan Welton, Jim Goll, Barbie Breathitt, and Praying Medic all have books about seeing in the spirit that I have enjoyed. Some have different opinions than I do on certain parts of the subject, but that is because we all come from different backgrounds and are approaching the subject from different angles. Maybe one of their books or teachings will fit your personality or answer your specific needs better than mine will.

As I said in earlier chapters, revelation transforms, and receiving from another person's revelation can transform you just as much as the revelations you discover for yourself.

Practice with a group.

I have said this before, but it bears repeating. Seeing in the spirit, along with every other spiritual gift I am familiar with, grows much faster when you partner with other people. Find or start a group that can practice together. Combine this key with the previous one, and start a group that reads through and discusses books and teachings about seeing in the spirit.

This is one of the reasons I love teaching at the Bethel Atlanta School of Supernatural Ministry. We get more than a hundred hungry people together two nights a week for nine months to pursue the deeper things of God. I haven't found a model that more greatly accelerates people into all God has for them, and I believe this is mostly due to the fact that we grow more quickly when we are running with, being challenged by, and partnering with others.

Cross-train.

The gifts of the Spirit are not islands; they are deeply connected to one another, and they are all rooted in God's nature. If you are getting nowhere in the realm of seeing in the spirit, then start chasing another gift. This is not because the gift of seeing in the spirit is not available to you—maybe you are just more naturally gifted in another area. I find that growth in one gift makes it much easier to grow in the others.

The prophetic is a natural place to start since it very strongly supports and is supported by seeing in the spirit. I recommend that if you want the gift of seeing in the spirit to be a major part of your life, you should devote equal time to pursuing the gift of prophecy. Thankfully there are wonderful teachers and books on the subject. Some of my favorite teachers are Kris Vallotton, Graham Cooke, and Shawn Bolz, all of whom have numerous books, teachings, and training materials.

Rest and realign.

Pursuing anything can grow exhausting over time, especially when you feel as if you are not experiencing success. Seeing in the spirit is not the most important thing for you to achieve in your lifetime; relationship with God is, and if your pursuit of any of His gifts is harming your connection with Him, then I recommend taking a break.

Go back to a place or activity where you felt connected with His presence. Spend time in worship. Spend time in the Word. Spend time with friends. Spend time with family. All these things are spiritual. God is present in all these things. Sometimes spending time in areas where we already experience peace or joy helps us reconnect to the source of all peace and joy.

Remember the Purpose

I cannot see in the spirit because I am a gifted person. I can see in the spirit because I have a heavenly Father who wants me to know Him. That is why I can see in the spirit; that is why you can see in the spirit. If there is anything you walk away with from this book, let it be this: God wants to know and be known by you.

I love seeing angels. I love watching how heaven responds when God's children worship Him. I love watching people be healed from sickness and disease. I love watching people step into their destiny. But I love these things because they belong to and come from my Father. In learning about them, I am learning about Him.

The most prominent seer in the New Testament was also the disciple that laid his head upon Jesus' chest. John, the author of the Book of Revelation, which is full of some of the most dramatic examples of heavenly visions and angelic encounters, also authored some of the most beautiful statements about God's love. He even called himself the disciple that Jesus loved. Our ability to see in the spirit, to see the world the way God does, is rooted in our intimacy with Him.

I want everyone to see in the spirit because I want everyone to see the Father and see what He is doing. That is what makes seeing in the spirit and every other gift of the Spirit worth pursuing. These gifts equip us to see what He is doing and do what He is doing. What greater joy could there be than to walk in the footsteps of a Father as good as ours?

SEEING-IN-THE-SPIRIT TRAINING—
DAY 7,367

TODAY I AM SITTING AT the Bethel Atlanta offices in Tyrone, Georgia. I have been part of the church and school of ministry here for ten years now, helping to build a culture that releases heaven on earth and equips people to continue in the style of ministry Jesus modeled for us. I am resting in a far corner of our open office, putting the finishing touches on my new book, *Profound Good*.

Our worship director and head sound engineer are talking over lunch, discussing the technical needs of the worship team in the upcoming budget year. An angel wearing crisply pressed white and gold robes and a pair of small golden reading glasses stands behind our sound engineer, checking things off a checklist with a silver pen.

A second angel, wearing a robe that looks as if it is made of multicolored flowing water, is standing behind the worship director. The angel drifts back and forth, moving to the rhythm of a song I cannot hear. Everything about it is constantly moving, not out of anxiety or impatience but as if it cannot help but make even the act of standing still into a form of worship.

A wind rises from behind both angels as the two people continue their conversation. Some of the water of the worship angel's robe is blown forward into the space between the two people. A fine golden dust is blown off the angel with the checklist, forming a shimmering cloud that drifts into the center. The water and gold dust mix, forming together into a broad sheet of translucent paper, with golden etchings and diagrams neatly filling every available corner. My immediate impression is of technical schematics or blueprints.

I recognize the angel standing behind our worship director as a worship angel because I have been seeing them for decades, and though they vary greatly in appearance, they all turn every little movement into an act of worship. I recognize the clipboard angel as one carrying the gift of administration. I have not been seeing these as long as I have been seeing worship angels, but I have seen them enough times to recognize the air of order and structure exemplified by their neat clothing and precise manner. They are not stiff or stodgy—in fact, they somehow carry their supreme excellence without displaying even a hint of perfectionism.

I recognize and understand the angels because of many years of practice and experience. I know the wind, and the subsequent movement of the water and gold dust, is a picture of what those angels are helping release. I have never seen anything exactly like what happened with the water and gold dust. Knowing the season our church is in—preparing for the groundbreaking of the new building on our recently purchased property—gives me some clue as to the purpose of those golden schematics.

When I hold the full picture in my mind—two different angels, a wind blowing, a piece of each angel merging to form something new—I feel heaven empowering cooperation between worship and administration. The angels are releasing heaven's grace to have two different gifts, two different sets of values, and two different sets of needs benefit each other rather than be at odds with each other.

I listen in on the conversation for a few minutes. Our worship director is talking about how to grow and expand what we do in worship when we move to our brand-new facility. Our head sound engineer is listing the best gear and setup to accommodate what the worship director is looking to build.

There are a dozen more people spread across our open office space. There are more than a dozen more angels blessing, protecting, supporting, and releasing various things all across the room. I could lean in with my attention and learn about what each of those angels is doing and how best to cooperate with it. It would probably take most of the day, I probably wouldn't get any other work done, and there would be a whole new set of things to see and learn tomorrow...and the next day...and the next.

I am still learning how to see in the spirit, and I believe I always will be. The brief portion I just shared may seem relatively straightforward, but there are still so many things I do not understand about even that small exchange.

Why was the checklist angel wearing glasses? What possible use could he have for those? Why did he have a checklist? What was he checking off? Why was the worship angel wearing clothes made of flowing water? Why was it a gust of wind that caused what the angels were carrying to merge?

It can feel overwhelming—the immensity of all that is happening in the spirit at every moment and in every place. How can I know which details are important and which are inessential? How do I know where to spend my limited time? How do I know which things I should respond to and which I should trust to God's divine plan?

These questions weigh me down when I focus on using my gift to benefit others or when I try to understand how the spirit world works. These questions fill me with excitement and joy when I focus on using my gift to get to know my Father better and then invite others into that relationship.

When the main goal is to benefit others, I do not know how much detail to give, how much background to explain, and how frequently I should share the things I see. When the main goal is to understand the spirit realm, I do not know which details are important, I get overwhelmed at how intricate and complex the spirit realm is, and I can almost never figure out how to derive anything useful from the things I see. When the goal is to learn more about my Father, I look for how every detail points back to His nature, I pull from a history of intimacy and connection to create a context for new things I see, and I am always excited to share a new layer of His goodness when I see it for the first time.

Seeing in the spirit only makes sense and produces good fruit when intimacy with God, the pursuit of His face, is at the very center of its purpose. We see in the spirit so we can see what He is doing. We see in the spirit so we can see what He is ready to do. We see in the spirit so we can see Him.

I have seen His face fifteen times since that Sunday morning at our church. I see it whenever I have the courage to look. I am beginning to suspect He never leaves at all.

ENDNOTES

The Quiz

1. Bethel School of Supernatural Ministry, accessed September 17, 2018, http://bssm.net/.

Activation and Study—Revelation

1. *Oxford American Dictionary*, 3rd ed. (Oxford, England: Oxford University Press, 2010), s.v. "revelation."

BLAKE K. HEALY, AUTHOR OF *Profound Good* and *The Veil*, is the director of the Bethel Atlanta School of Supernatural Ministry. At BASSM Blake and his team train revivalists who hear the voice of God, know their heavenly identity, and operate with supernatural power and authority. If you would like to grow in the prophetic ministry, see signs, wonders, and miracles, learn more about seeing in the Spirit, and grow closer to your heavenly Father than ever before, then visit bethelatlantaschool.com for more information or to apply for the upcoming school year.

Your life will never be the same.